FACES OF THE LIVING DEAD

FACES OF
THE LIVING DEAD

The stories behind
the amazing psychic art
of
Frank Leah

by

Paul Miller

First published in 1943

re-published in collaboration with
Psychic Press (1995) Ltd
www.psychicnewsbookshop.co.uk
by
Saturday Night Press Publications
York, England
snppbooks@gmail.com

ISBN 978-0-9557050-5-2

Printed by
Lightning Source
www.lightningsource.com

Frank Leah

a dedicated servant of Spirit who passed
to the Higher Life in 1972

Contents

List of Illustrations

Drawings and Photographs   Page

Introduction

It is with the greatest pleasure that I write this introduction to the new edition of *Faces of the Living Dead*, Paul Miller's detailed account of the work of a unique medium, which has been far too long out of print.

Frank Leah was by any standards the greatest psychic artist this world has seen. A journalist, draughtsman, artist and sculptor by profession, he was art editor and cartoonist to five Dublin journals, later moving to work in London's Fleet Street. He became a willing and devoted servant of the Spirit World as its inhabitants sought to prove through his outstanding mediumistic and artistic gifts that they had survived beyond the change called death and were very much alive in a new environment just as real, if not more so, than our own.

Leah hated the word 'dead' being applied to his Spirit visitors because he insisted that they were vibrantly alive. They were not phantoms who bore resemblance to the conventional idea of ghosts. To him they were as natural and normal as the people he met in the street.

Featured regularly in *Psychic News* over a period of some forty years, Frank Leah also became known within the pages of mainstream publications. Not only did he provide the ultimate visual evidence of survival, he frequently conveyed startlingly accurate clairvoyant and clairaudient information to his sitters while he drew. Highly evidential to those sitters was the fact that he frequently took on, in painful replication, the last physical experiences of those Spirit people who presented themselves to be portrayed. "I have died over a thousand deaths," he once said.

Sometimes the characteristics in a portrait were at first denied by a recipient – until they did some research. The comparison photograph invariably produced after Leah completed a portrait often revealed facial peculiarities which had long been forgotten. Files in the *Psychic News* archive contain scores of documented cases where, following such research, original photographs were unearthed which bore witness to the accuracy of the Spirit portrait, in some cases long after Leah had completed the drawing.

Read and enjoy the astonishing evidence of one who left his sitters in no doubt that the Spirit people are very much alive, as we all will be when our time comes to leave this earth. Time and again parents have identified their children, husbands and wives their partners of many decades in portraits drawn by Frank Leah. The comparison photos later provided by those who were fortunate to receive Spirit portraits from Leah say it all. There can be no mistaking the extraordinary likenesses inspired by those in Spirit who were determined to bring comfort to those from whom, for a brief time, they were separated by physical death.

From my first sight of a rare copy of Paul Miller's book it has been my cherished aim to make it available to the public once again. I record my grateful thanks to Ann Harrison of Saturday Night Press, whose efforts in producing this new edition have been immense. Her enthusiasm for seeing this extraordinary testament to the power of Spirit returned to its rightful place in the world's bookshops has matched my own. My thanks go also to Magnus Smith of *Psychic News*, whose expertise has ensured the optimum clarity of the old photographs which are key to this book. Finally, I thank the anonymous donor who put his money where his mouth was and made this new edition possible.

Susan Farrow

Editor, Psychic News

Stansted, April 2010

1

Faces of The Living Dead

"If only I could see his face." That is the heart-cry of the mourner from the moment the body is laid away until time wears down the sharp edge of grief – or until Spiritualism answers the cry and there appears in reality the voice, the touch, the message, or the face of the living dead. It has happened so often that the time has come to record, in lasting form, some of the many cases of evidence which prove, beyond question, that not only do the 'dead' live beyond the grave, but that they have the power, under suitable conditions and with the right kind of medium, to pose for their portraits.

Unfortunately for the armies of mourners throughout the world, there is only one medium trained to draw or paint the 'dead'. This is his story – Frank Leah, a journalist, artist and medium. He was born with the psychic gift he now employs for the comfort of mourners. Long before he understood its meaning and purpose he was afraid of it. He sees with the eye of the Spirit in a special way, for we all have some degree of perception. In most it is buried beneath the cares of the day and of this world; in others its beholding is ignored or dismissed as day-dreams. To others again, as in Leah's case, it flowers as an artistic gift which is employed for a great and beneficent work – the stilling of fear, the soothing of the brooding mind, the comforting of the aching heart, and the kindling of the joy of recollection of the face of the well-known and well-beloved.

Now a psychic or spiritual gift has to be trained. It is not something handed to the medium and left untended. The greater the technical skill in the medium, the greater the service that is done, for those who from the Other Side have charge of this work can then impress their points of evidence with greater skill and ease. Behind every evidential drawing, behind every detail impressed on paper, there is a story. Those who, from the Spirit World, guide this medium-artist are so well versed in their work that they neglect nothing that will bring conviction – but when they have reached that point they go no further. That is a fact. Leah has given hundreds of instances of it. Did they so desire, I have no doubt – because of my long acquaintance with the power of those who guide mediums – the Spirit operators could paint pictures that would rival the best in our art galleries. Often they are the great painters and singers, poets and musicians, teachers and reformers, doing again their familiar work from another place. That is all, and they temper their power to their purpose. They show in another form, a form all can understand, that there is no death, that the body perishes and the soul lives on, retaining memories, affections and the power to show facial peculiarities, aye, and even blemishes, for evidential purposes. The warm human personalities are alive always; and as of old they like to comfort those they love and have left behind. They like to know they have succeeded in catching the artist's eye, and that he has put their likenesses on record.

In the early days of Leah's work he received sitters, all anonymously, through Spiritualist societies, and for their satisfaction he used a red torch to light his drawing board and paper while he worked, always with the sitter as close to him as possible.

Leah has had many kinds of sitters. Many know nothing of Survival until they come to him. It would make no difference to him if he used a red torch or an electric light, for many of the drawings are made in his mind – if not, in fact, on paper – before the sitters arrive. Sometimes he describes the 'dead' on the telephone before the prospective sitter has had time to give a name and ask for an appointment. How could Leah know who was going to telephone him – unless the 'dead' relative told him? Some spirits are drawn in daylight; others have been done on the top deck of a London bus.

Here is an instance of how he works. Recently Leah was on all-night A.R.P. duty and he came home to his little London flat-studio, very tired, late the following morning. He sat down intending to rest a little and wait for the morning post before having a bath. He had no intention of sleeping in the chair. But suddenly he dozed off. For three minutes he was asleep. While his body rested his mind was alive, and he saw a man, vivid and clear, who told his story, and said that his daughter was going to telephone for an appointment shortly. Half an hour later there was a telephone call, and when Leah answered, he said he knew what the caller wanted; that she was coming in the hope that her father would appear for his portrait. He told her it would be done; that her father had been to the studio – and he gave a description of him and his business association with her. Now, how do you explain that, except on the basis that what is written here and what is shown here is true? There can be no other satisfactory explanation. The 'dead' men and women say so. Their relatives say so. The artist says so. And now I say so. There is no other record like this in the world. There is no other artist doing quite the same work – yet. Therefore it is a fact to say that this work is unique in the world of Spiritualism and in the world of art. The technical merit is there. In some cases it is brilliant. The evidence is there. It but remains to present the case to the widest public that they should benefit.

In the first instance all the sketches are outlined rapidly, though not all are completed rapidly. Some are finished within a few minutes; some have been done in a few seconds. Yet other spirits are obstinate or retiring, and the work is retarded or complicated. Often a life-size head will appear so rapidly that it seems not to be drawn but to be projecting itself on the paper. Yet it is being done in this great city of London. You do not have to travel to the East to see this wonder. It is done by a British artist, who lives a simple life alone, dedicated to this work. He lives it, for in him often there are reproduced the pains of the passing of those who return for the first time to show that they are alive and not the 'dead' who are mourned. The artist claims nothing. All the statements on recognition and likeness come from the relatives of those who appear from the Spirit World. Then the sitters produce their photographs. Leah does not see any photographs before he does the drawings, for as you have read, often they are done before he meets the sitter. He does not need the photographs, except for comparison – afterwards.

Nothing like this beneficent work of Spiritualism is done in any other way. The churches do not do it. They cannot, for they have driven out the power of the Spirit and have substituted for it the creed and the ritual, the dogma and the catechism, the vestment and the orders; and for the voice of the Spirit they have the voice of Orthodoxy. There is no inspired hand in vestry or in cathedral that draws one line of the faces of the living dead. Theirs is the work of dead dogma. No creed can bring back the voice you knew and the face you knew. There is no substitute for evidence. There is nothing to replace fact, and there is no fact that can die.

It is always relatives of the living dead who are enthusiastic about the Leah drawings. They know. Leah actually sees the spirits who pose for their portraits. He sees them as a sculptor sees a finished model – that is they have length, breadth and thickness. It is a feeling akin to being able to walk round a living person, taking shape and proportions without a single movement on the part of the communicator. It is common for a good likeness to be made in half a minute. One excellent drawing was done in nine seconds. There are others which take much longer. One exceptional case took nine years from the first outlines to the completed details. As the artist is at work he has no sensation of time. He is absorbed in his task, and is always fascinated with the eagerness of spirits to show themselves evidentially. Sometimes they insist on displaying blemishes, even little moles that have been skilfully removed from the face.

Now this artist is besieged by people who want drawings of their 'dead' husbands, wives, brothers, sisters and friends. He could go on without rest for the next fifty years, and he looks about in vain for a sign of the appearance of another artist who will take up similar work. But mediums are born, and then they are trained; and they are all different. Even so, the public now interested in the living dead has grown so that Leah is fully employed. He has given up everything for it. It is the kind of evidence you cannot forget or argue away. You could not, for example, demonstrate or argue that it was due to telepathy, for how could a man working in a dim light draw the face of someone he had not seen? It is easy for an artist to draw some kind of a face – if he does not care about the result, but even where no likeness is intended, there is usually a model.

So, how can anyone explain away this extraordinary faculty? It is more rational to accept the results of the artist's vision – that he sees those whom he draws – than it is to invent a theory. The artist's work, moreover, has the corroboration in the millions of cases of proved Survival. The spirits who elsewhere speak in the direct voice, or write through the hand of a medium, or show themselves to the clairvoyant sight, can just as readily pose for their portraits. They come for one reason – to prove that they live on, that the grave is not the end, and that they have a loving, beneficent mission to fulfil in comforting those they leave behind.

Not only does Leah see the 'dead', but he hears them as well, and it is they who tell him of their relationship to those who come to him for sittings. No people on earth are as courteous as the 'dead', none so considerate. They have every reason to be patient. They are living in eternity and come as visitors to this world where we have so little time to spare. The 'dead' often come to him when he is talking on the telephone, and start their evidence then. They are the eager ones. They are anxious to impress their likenesses on the artist's memory. They seek out their friends, and they are the happiest when they prove themselves. They live in a world of reality. They can see the effects of causes, and they know beyond a doubt that one heart comforted is worth more than all the sermons in the world, and that there is nothing greater than truth. That is the all-impelling motive and purpose behind Spirit return. There is nothing else, for when the primary purpose of Survival is demonstrated, all other facts follow, and they are many. This is a great work, and it fulfils itself in many ways. There is no limit to the good it can do, and there is none who cannot benefit from it. It is a healing work in the widest sense, for when the soul is touched the restorative forces at the command of the Spirit are released, and the greater task of self-expression begins.

It is true of all mediums who are well-trained and give evidence of this kind that they have more work to do than they can manage and, in spite of the very common informer and the ignorant and spiteful attacks of the enemies of Spiritualism, the evidence is given. Seldom nowadays do people who have thought, even slightly, of Spiritualism laugh or sneer at it. That is left to those with a vested interest to serve – either religious or scientific. Nearly all those who inquire become convinced, until now there is a growing consciousness right across the world that only through the efforts of Spiritualists, and the indispensable mediums, there is an awareness of life beyond the grave, and that those who pass on can and do return to prove their Survival and leave on record for centuries, if needed, their portraits.

When we consider how rapidly, for the most part, these psychic likenesses are drawn, we must also remember that when a non-psychic artist – even of world repute – has a sitter for an hour at a time, the portrait may take weeks and even months, to finish. The desired likeness for a basis of the non-psychical artist's work does not always appear at the first or even third sitting, That factor, when considered alongside the high speed – nearly as fast as photography – of Leah's work, should be taken into account when we see that the whole aim is not to present a work for the Royal Academy, but to show a likeness of someone who is not visible to normal sight, someone who has not been seen by the artist in normal life. I know that this may sound like repetition, but unless the case is clearly outlined at the start we will have to make this point again and again.

Mourners, of course, unless they are experts, are seldom interested in the technicalities of the work. Their sole concern is to see again the face of the one they love. It is the purpose of this book to show that this happens; that the portraits are evidential there is no doubt, for the living vouch for the faces of the 'dead'. What then is left? Only that we should spread the good news over all the world so that other aching hearts may be lightened; that other minds may be rescued from the darkness of ignorance bred by false teaching throughout the ages. We are the inheritors not only of knowledge but of ignorance. The force of ignorance is great. It raises itself up against the seekers after truth everywhere. There is but one means of destroying it. And those who seek to spread this priceless knowledge of life after death, which kills only ignorance and liberates the human mind, are few.

Mediums are not found every day. They are all different because they are trained by Spirit guides who think long over the work their instruments have to carry out. Training is a long process. In some cases it continues from childhood almost up to middle age. Guides do the best they can with the mediums they have. Always there is a shortage of mediums; always there are thousands of people seeking their services. Therefore, through books like this it is the hope that we shall achieve three things – to prove the worth of another medium who gives irrefutable evidence of the life after death; comfort the mourner; and encourage others to serve as Leah has served and is serving.

Until you know something of the vast organisation on the Other Side that keeps us supplied with evidence, you might think, as most inquirers do, that it all just happens, and that everything is the result of fortuitous circumstances uncontrolled by anything save the needs of the moment. But experience finds it otherwise. And some of the best-known guides, those who are experts in helping the 'dead' to prove their survival, say that there has to be much preparation before a sitting. Some of the evidence is prepared a long time ahead, yet most of it is presented to give the appearance of spontaneity. It does not mean that the communicator is, like most of our dull broadcasters, reading something from a script. You know the kind of thing – "Ah, Captain Bellbottoms, have you been long at sea?" "Yes, I have been at sea, man and boy for thirty-five years." "You must have had a good many adventures?" "Oh, yes, I have had a good many adventures." "Won't you tell us something about them?" Then the Captain reads something of his life-story, not in his own words, but in language provided for him, and his relatives say: "Well, that's not old Bellbottoms, anyway. He doesn't talk like that."

Now in the séance room, or in the studio where the 'dead' have their portraits drawn, there is preparation, but the communicators, when they use their own voices, speak as they are accustomed to. You never hear a Cockney talking with an Oxford accent; you do not hear a man who never looked through a telescope talking about the vast interstellar spaces. It is all so natural. If the mourner seeking evidence is slow in the uptake, the spirits do not become impatient as we do. They understand it is new; often the difficulty is to restrain the eager Spirit who in his joy at reunion wants to pour out all his love and gladness in one short sitting. Sometimes there are tears of happiness that the veil is at last broken; sometimes there are loving words spoken in the accents of gladness common to those who truly meet again after a long separation or after a trying experience.

You have to know the séance room well, you have to experience the work of many guides and mediums before you understand even a little of the great amount of work that has to be done before one piece of evidence is successfully presented. Not all sitters are equally helpful. Some put up the barriers of grief, some cling to their fears that this is something that should not be done, and others are afraid because they do not know. The fact remains that in innumerable cases there is successful communication, and after the first errors of eagerness and fear, the communion between the 'dead' and ourselves takes the rightful and natural place it must have in the life of any truly civilised world.

It is the fact of greatest moment in the world. Without it all our hopes are vain, we may plan a score of new worlds, and have no certainty that they will endure unless we have the conviction based on evidence that there is a continuing life beyond this; and for which this is a preparation.

The Spirit guides do not desire to receive into their care ignorant men and women and children. It has long been their complaint that the kind of people we send over from our world have to be re-educated. They pass hence knowing either nothing of the state in which they are to dwell for all eternity – or with the crudest man-made ideas about purgatory, angels playing harps and a vengeful deity waiting to punish them for things that an ordinary father would forgive almost as soon as they were done.

It is because they want better citizens of this world and of the next that the guides have raised up mediums of the Leah type. They want to spread the knowledge that makes men free of their fears. They want us to remake our lives in the certain knowledge that we are planning for an enduring purpose; that when we pass hence we will retain our interests; that the skill acquired here in this world will not perish with our bodies, but that it will remain with our affections, and that we will be able to employ all the qualities we have evolved in co-operative effort between the two worlds.

2

Proof in Nine Seconds

Probably one of the fastest drawings in the world was done by Leah during a visit to Norwich in 1937. He had a three-day engagement to take a Spiritualist service, give a lantern lecture on his work, and do portraits. He was told that twelve sittings were booked for him, and that one woman, a Mrs. Burgess, wanted to see him urgently at her home. She did not go out much because of her deafness. A Spirit voice told the artist to leave Mrs. Burgess to the last. The stranger to Spiritualism soon realises that when a Spirit takes the trouble to tell a medium to do something, it is for a good reason, though not always one that appears immediately. There has to be the closest co-operation and absolute trust between medium and guide before work like this is done.

And Leah's Spirit voice asked him to go to Mrs. Burgess last – it is shown – because her 'dead' mother wanted to give her a present. The present was the nine-second sketch – and a good deal of evidence that members of the Burgess family were not only alive beyond the veil, but were actively interested in proving themselves.

This is Leah's story: "I went to Mrs. Burgess' house in the Crescent, about a mile away. I was dead beat. The weather was vile, and I resented having to walk through it and getting drenched as a preliminary to doing a job of this kind. And yet, having dropped my dripping things in Mrs. Burgess' hall, I set to work at once, and the portrait of her husband was done, Mrs.

Burgess being seated at my side. I should explain that I saw her communicator neither objectively nor subjectively, as I usually do. His face was clearly outlined on my drawing paper, a fact I pointed out to Mrs. Burgess. But she, alas, could not see it. There was, therefore, little left for me to do but fill in the features. I have often had this experience, but never before have I portrayed a communicator so swiftly, the previous record being a quarter of a minute for a life-size portrait." This Burgess drawing is four inches deep, and was completed in five minutes, although the preliminary sketch took only nine seconds.

Leah obtained much clairvoyant evidence for Mrs. Burgess, whose husband he found had been a doctor before passing in 1919. Mrs. Burgess' brother, also a doctor, appeared. He passed in 1906. The mother showed herself 'wearing a white cap and weepers very similar to those worn by Queen Victoria'. The artist roughed in her features, but soon found that she had not come to be drawn. Her visit was to celebrate the anniversary of her 'death'. She wanted to give her daughter an appropriate gift. And had succeeded. That, says the artist, is why he was told by the Spirit voice to leave his appointment with Mrs. Burgess to the last. It was left so late that she had almost given up hope of seeing him.

3

Two Husbands Prove Their Survival to One Wife

What happens when a woman who had two husbands passes over? That question is often asked of Spiritualists. One answer is that where the bond of attraction is strongest it will operate, but there is every reason why all three should be friends. There is no longer any difference over possession or the exclusive right to anyone's company when you leave this world. But here, through the mediumship of Leah, is a case where the two husbands of one woman returned at the same séance and posed for their portraits.

Both men had something that distinguished them, and Leah captured these little things and put them on record. In one instance the artist saw what the widow had forgotten. She could hardly be blamed for that, because her first husband had 'died' twenty-five years before, and it is not likely that she would remember every detail. But the artist was right, and that point alone shows that you can rule out telepathy. For if telepathy is the explanation, then mediums have developed it to a remarkable degree, while those who claim that it explains all phenomena of this kind have not made the slightest progress with their theory since they first put it forward. Usually, when a man discovers a law or a force in nature he is able to do something about it. History has many such cases, but nothing in the history of Spiritualism shows that anyone has come within a million miles of explaining the facts except on the basis that it all happens as we say – the 'dead' return to prove they are not dead, and with the aid of Spirit guides show considerable ingenuity in doing so. Take this series of portraits as an example.

Mrs. Ethel Gibbon, of Sussex Gardens, west London, made her first appointment with Leah anonymously, and when she saw him it was for the first time in her life. If you know Leah's quick, direct way of speaking you can imagine him saying this as he did to Mrs. Gibbon almost as soon as she entered the room: "There are two husbands here, but the second husband comes more strongly." Then the Spirit gave the medium his name as Hugh, adding that he was a doctor. His full name was Alfred Hugh Gibbon. He explained that he had come to 'collect' his wife's mother who was being prepared for her passing. He told Leah that his mother-in-law had lived on the Other Side for many months, though still on earth, and that she was 102. Now the artist, accustomed to making portraits, could not believe that, and he said so because the daughter who was in the room with him did not look as though her mother was anything like a hundred years old.

Then the doctor posed for his portrait, showing himself wearing a monocle in his left eye. This was confirmed on comparison with a normal photograph. He also showed himself with his cigarette holder as a further proof of his identity. The whole drawing took two minutes, but it was not the end of the evidence for Mrs. Gibbon, for the artist prophesied that her mother would pass within a month. True, a prophecy is not evidence until it comes to pass, but this one did.

Leah, some time later, saw clairvoyantly the passing of Mrs. Gibbon's mother. When the daughter came for a second sitting he told her this, and added that her mother was present then and would have her portrait done. The old woman told Leah that if she had remained on earth for another month she would have been 103. That was admitted to be correct. Leah could not believe even now that his Spirit visitor had lived so long, for her abundant hair still had colour in it, and she appeared to him no more than an alert woman of eighty. But he drew what he saw

– an old lady wearing her favourite shawl – and the finished portrait is similar to a press picture on her 102nd birthday.

There was still more evidence for, as soon as this drawing was done, the medium saw Mrs. Gibbon's first husband, who had 'died' twenty-five years before. When that drawing was done Mrs. Gibbon said that although she recognised it as being her first husband, the side-whiskers were a little too long and the moustache not large enough, for he always wore his moustache deep to cover his rather prominent teeth. But when the psychic sketch was compared with a normal photograph, it was seen that the clairvoyant's sight was better than the wife's memory, for the side whiskers and moustache were just as they were drawn.

Now here are sufficient facts for the sceptics and for the inquirers to ponder over. It could not have been done by telepathy, for the wife said that her first husband's side whiskers and moustache were not as the artist drew them, but she was proved wrong. And if it is a case of telepathy, why did the medium persist in his view that the old lady he saw was about eighty, when, in fact, she was 102? These are only some of the points, without adding the complication that the woman did not say she had two husbands when she went for the first sitting. How do you 'telepath' that? I don't know, but it is not our purpose to follow the endless maze of theory. I am presenting the facts, and these are striking enough.

When critics jeer at fortune-telling and confuse it with Spiritualism, and when they talk of 'back-parlour' séances as though we were still in the Victorian era and the public knew nothing about our case, they forget or ignore the vast body of factual knowledge that has been built up. This knowledge is as factual as anything in physics. All of it is verifiable. It all has the backing of human testimony, and though the mental phenomena cannot be reproduced at will in a laboratory as some researchers would wish, similar phenomena can be produced, provided the conditions are right, and in the end they demonstrate that the same fundamental law operates.

We do not come before the world with a case that causes a stir for a few days and then is forgotten. We have something to demonstrate to reasonable men and women that will endure as long as there are aching hearts and minds in doubt about the Great Beyond. Out of such human incidents as the one I have just quoted our case is built. All séances differ, just as we all change from day to day, but the main characteristics remain, the same trend of thought, and that gives the Spiritualist case half its attraction – its infinite variety. There is no need to fear that it will pall; that you will grow weary of the same thing. It does not happen like that. Behind the veil there are hosts of sentient, warm beings whose mission is to help mankind, often the mankind they have not long left. They retain their affection for progress, their love of justice, their burning eagerness to see wrongs righted, and to bring the light of a nobler mode of life into this world in which so much beauty is obscured by so much ignorance.

If it is in my power, I would like to show you that there is a vast beneficent organisation composed of well-wishers and well-doers. The men who were skilled here in the separation of the false from the true do not lose that faculty because they lose a body that answers ill to the quick needs of the human spirit. Those whom you knew, and countless others whom you did not know, are allied together for nothing less than the regeneration of the whole human family of nations and races.

They know nothing of the barriers of class and caste in their work. They see all men and women and children and animals as parts of the Great Spirit of all life striving for expression. They see that there are sufficient difficulties imposed by the war of physical and spiritual evolution without adding to them the manacles and the shackles of manmade reaction.

The spread of this knowledge – which rids us of our fears and restores the trials of daily life to their proper place – is restricted only by the lack of instruments we call mediums. There are other instruments, too, the reformers, the inventors, the pioneers in all fields of human work. As they make themselves ready for the inflow of inspiration, so does humanity feel the upward pull of the evolving spirit; so do men in the dark places of the earth take new heart after each failure and strive anew for the coming of the brighter day – if not for themselves then for their children and the nations that are to come after us.

We present to the world a picture of a vast, evolving universe with all that is needed and nothing neglected. We show that there is a beneficent purpose; we reveal that there is no soul, however lowly in the eyes of men, who has not his great and imperishable value to the scheme that needs also the tides and the seasons and the little things of field and forest. It is with that as our background, revealed throughout almost a century of Spiritualism, that we here present the simple facts on which the whole edifice rests. These facts are shown by masters in the art of presenting evidence to be related to the grand whole that gives a new confidence to everyone who leaves the séance room with the tears of mourning wiped away.

In that light, consider this instance of evidence given through Leah's mediumship. In much less time than it takes to set the type from which this page is printed, Leah drew seven portraits of Percy George Stocker, who had 'died' eighteen years before. Five of the seven sketches took thirty seconds each. They all came unsought. Not all came together, yet they form a record of a boy who became a mature man. Fortunately, the Stocker family kept photographs, so we can compare the psychic drawings with them. The sitting at which the drawings were completed was given to Stocker's wife and daughter, and they were so thrilled with the portrayal of him at different stages of his life, and with the force of other evidence which Stocker gave clairaudiently to the artist, that they forgot to take full notes.

One of the highly evidential points is the artist's indication of the deep groove in Stocker's forehead in at least two sketches. Stocker often amused friends by holding coins in this groove. Mrs. Stocker and her daughter, without telling each other, had the strongest impression to arrange a sitting with Leah, whom they had not previously met. At the first séance not only did Stocker show himself to the artist, but he also gave much evidence. He traced for his wife and daughter two routes from the hall at which the séance was held to his old home in south-west London. They were confused because he spoke of the front door of his house opening first to the left and then to the right. This was a good point of evidence, because Stocker had lived in two houses in turn, next door to each other, and the front doors opened different ways. This obviously lively man showed himself with his hair being pulled over his face. His wife and daughter said that was one of his mannerisms. He mentioned the date of his wedding, of his daughter's birthday, and said that his passing was unexpected and sudden, and that it was caused by pneumonia. The Spirit proved, as many others have done, that their memories are better than ours, for he reminded his wife that he formerly wore a link watch chain, which she had forgotten.

Mother and daughter left the séance room happy, but though they were satisfied, apparently Stocker was not, for he asked for another meeting, and a fortnight later the medium drew a large portrait showing a man of about fifty-two, that is, a few years before he passed on. In this portrayal the parting of the hair was correctly shown; even the colour of the eyes was given and a slight peculiarity in the eyebrows. Stocker recalled his childhood, and mentioned the word 'marbles'. Though Mrs. Stocker knew him at the time of which he spoke, she could not remember anything to do with marbles. But later she recalled that, as a boy, he was very fond of the game of solitaire, which is played with marbles. And he nearly always won. Perhaps that is why he remembered long after his wife had forgotten.

Now you must remember that the drawings are done almost in the dark, that the artist has nothing to model his likeness on – except the living dead as they show themselves to him. No one, no organisation in the world could keep track of all the peculiarities which this active and eager Spirit displayed as he stood on the far side of death and showed himself as he was through the seven ages from boyhood to mature manhood. There is no drama like the truth as revealed in the séance room; there is no fiction half so interesting; and there is no knowledge so lasting.

4
Five Years' Wait for Recognition

The preceding was a case where all the normal photographs were kept and where comparison was instantaneous. But here is a case in which the medium, when he did the first of two drawings, forecast that it would take five years to find a photograph for comparison with it. He was right. The first picture showed the mother of Miss F. V. Gregory as she looked just about the time her daughter was born. Later Leah saw the 'dead' woman as she appeared at the age of seventy-two. Miss Gregory did have a photograph for comparison. The second portrait was drawn in one minute.

I can surmise, I think fairly, from these two instances, that given the artist-medium's working speed it would be as easy for the Spirit guides to produce a drawing of every person who passes over as it is for us here to have a photograph taken. And it is often quicker apparently to have your 'dead' friends drawn by a medium than it is to have a picture taken.

Though this is the most solemn of all truth, not all that happens in the séance room is unlit by laughter, and sometimes those who come back want us to know that they still laugh at jokes. Some of them even try out their humour on us, and though we cannot always appreciate the points they make, it is additional evidence that they are the same people with the same sense of humour. There are others who show their old skill in witticisms linked with topical events. So witty are some of these remarks that when they are tried on non-Spiritualists I am always asked "Who said that?" Of course when they hear it is someone who has 'died', you can almost see on their faces the thought: "If I had known, I might not have said it was funny." Of course, not all human beings are so mean-spirited, but the fact remains that the 'dead', as well as the living, like to make us laugh, like to raise the appreciative smile, and like to be thought adept at making the kind of sallies that ease the tension of any serious gathering.

Here is an example of the retention of human characteristics. Thomas N. Tunbridge was a conductor of orchestras. At one time he conducted the orchestra at Daly's Theatre under George Edwardes. He was a jolly man and showed his nature by insisting on a caricature of himself, with a cigar in his mouth, being done by Leah. Not spiritual, the cynics may say. But it is more evidential than if he showed himself with a harp. He liked cigars, and when he appeared the medium said the room seemed to be full of cigar smoke. Then, when he had had his fun, Tunbridge, who came to prove himself to his wife, posed for a serious portrait. He indicated his profession by waving his hands as conductors do. While Tunbridge was showing himself the medium had a vision of his passing. The musician was driving a car. There was an accident, and he was thrown through the windscreen. But he did not return to bemoan his passing. He was anxious to have a caricature of himself with his beloved cigar, and then he passed to the serious work of posing for a portrait.

I said earlier that there was infinite variety in the evidence for Survival, and all reasonable people who have read so far must admit that there has been a good deal of variety already. You would think the guides and those who desire to prove their identities would soon reach the limit of their ingenuity in presenting their facts. But we all have at least one story to tell, and though in the end it amounts to the same thing, the telling is different, and the details are arranged differently in all our lives. Besides, in the Spirit World they never choose people for what they say they are; they have to prove their ability.

Not all those who return have the same light-hearted story to tell. Here is an instance in which the name is not given for reasons that appear immediately. A woman sat with Leah. Her father appeared, and it was stated that he showed himself as he was just before he committed suicide by poisoning himself as his wife lay dying in the next room. Then he appeared as he was fifty years before his passing. The woman did not know how she could verify the portrait of her father as a young man because she had no photograph for comparison. But the medium said that someone in her family had a photograph that would do what she wanted. Some months later a photograph was found, and it is printed alongside the psychic drawing for comparison.

One evidential point, in addition to the drawings, and given by the Spirit, was that he married in Australia. This was correct. If the Spirit did not know there was a photograph of himself as a young man he could not have told his daughter. And since she did not know and had to look for it – or wait until it was found for her – there is no hope that the medium could have known, unless he was told by the only man who knew. That makes this kind of mediumship more than just drawing the faces of the 'dead'. They all prove themselves in their own way.

Here is an instance of a Persian Muslim appearing, writing his name in Persian, and mentioning Mecca to indicate that he was a follower of Mahomet. This communicator gave the name of the town Kierbeleh, near Baghdad, where his body was buried. After showing himself as he was normally, he gave a pose indicating the kind of illness he endured before passing by depicting himself with an ice-bag on his head. As he did so, Leah experienced a sharp pain between the eyes and ears.

Pride in personal appearance is not confined to us. Those who no longer have physical bodies like to appear at their most attractive – especially women. That is true of Mrs. Amy Hill, who showed herself as a full-faced woman of about thirty-five when her husband was with Leah. Now Mrs. Hill was seventy when she passed, but she insisted on showing herself as a young woman. Hill was puzzled by Leah's insistence that his wife's hair was parted in the centre. He said he knew it was wrong. Then the medium realised that what he saw was not a parting but a streak of white hair which shows clearly in both the psychic drawing and in the photograph with which it is compared. Mrs. Hill not only proved her survival by the white streak in her hair, but reminded her husband of their life together in southern India.

Here is yet another of the little things which, strung together, are woven into the vast tapestry of Spiritualist evidence that graces the hall of truth. Always it is the little things that count in the end, as in this case where the son of the communicator vouched for the facts which his father related to Leah. First the artist-medium saw a man dressed in frockcoat and silk hat and showing a buttonhole and rolled umbrella. He indicated that this was his normal dress. Leah could not make out his occupation, so the Spirit showed himself walking to work, removing his coat and silk hat, putting on a large apron and picking up hammers, chisels and saws. The communicator was a cabinet maker – probably the best-dressed cabinet maker of his time.

Once while drawing in the dark, Leah produced a striking drawing of a parson, the Rev. G. Gibson Gunn, M.A., whose daughter was in the room and recognised it as a perfect likeness. Again the Spirit organisers of this kind of evidence have introduced a novel touch by drawing a hat only in outline so as to leave the forehead visible for comparison with the photograph. If the spirits – or the 'dead' clergyman – did not know of the photograph showing the wide deep forehead, how could they have taken precautions to make that point in the drawing Leah was doing? It appears that they plan better than we do, though that is not to be wondered at, for there is very little of the right kind of planning in this world at any time. We are the imperfect improvisers – when it is nearly too late and sometimes when it is more than too late. Yet, even though they planned to show the characteristic forehead, the Spirit communicators did not forget that little extra piece of evidence of identity. This clergyman told the medium, which his daughter confirmed, that he went to school with Dr. Randall Davidson, who later became Archbishop of Canterbury.

An instance of a versatile man is John Millard, who was born 140 years before his great-grandson received his personal proof of Survival. John Millard impressed Leah with a vision of Glastonbury, and then indicated a farm twelve miles away, saying that he lived there. He not only played church organs but also built them. His novel piece of evidence was that he was a child of his mother's second marriage. He also said that he was born in 1797.

All these statements were confirmed by his great-grandson, who later gave Leah a photograph of his ancestor. It is clear from the style of the whiskers and beard alone that Leah must have seen before him what he drew. He could not imagine a likeness, and I do not see how even the miraculous telepathic faculty could be stretched from the artist's studio to the unknown spot in which the old photograph was kept. That ignores all the difficulties of impressing it on the medium's brain – or wherever it is that the telepathic faculty is alleged to operate in these cases where the evidence is so strong that the sceptics and the opponents have to find some argument when they have no reason on their side.

What would you do if a Spirit appeared in your studio while you were painting and gave you the name and address of a woman with whom he wished to communicate? This is what Leah did. He telephoned the address, but found that the woman named was out of town. So he did the drawing of the young man who had come unbidden and took it to the woman's companion, who at once identified it as that of a close friend of their early days. When the woman whose address was given – Mrs. Wood-Sims – returned to town a fortnight later, she produced the photograph which is printed along with the Spirit sketch. You have to bear in mind that when Leah did the drawing, the young man was a stranger to him, but his special piece of evidence is that he remembered the address of his friend. So he achieved recognition by two people.

Again a woman, by drawing attention to the style in which she wore her hair, proved her identity. She was Mrs. Ramsay, and she appeared to Leah as she had been some years before she 'died', her daughter could not recall her with her hair in that fashion. The medium assured the daughter that she would find a photograph to prove his statement. Nine months later the photograph was found, and the style of hair as drawn by the artist was confirmed.

Now, how did he know, if he did not see Mrs. Ramsay? It is as difficult to imagine a hairstyle as any other impossible thing in the world. No man could guess how a woman would have her hair done, and if he tried to imagine the favourite style of a stranger he would surely be wrong. In this case not even the woman's daughter remembered, so she could not 'telepath' what she did not know!

By now the reader should begin to appreciate that a convinced Spiritualist is difficult to shake off once he is set on demonstrating his evidence. There is, in every example of Leah's work, one outstanding fact or several. The fact may in itself be small in relation to the whole case, but fact, and important fact, it remains. The reader should by now also begin to feel that this case is being proved and that no theory can explain away the case for Survival. It has withstood all the tests scientists can devise, all the allegations of those who have not investigated – and they are by far the most vocal – and it has steadily beaten down all the ill-informed opposition.

Our facts have survived the best and the worst the opponents can work out. There have been fair investigations in which we have triumphed, and there have been pre-arranged 'exposures' which depended solely on cheating and sleight-of-hand for their success. Often the people who framed these affairs were, they imagined, motivated by the best intentions – to prove that we were wrong, but how two wrongs make a right is not explained. But where the investigators have set out to examine our case fairly, the almost invariable result has been to win a new supporter. Not all those who become convinced are ready to come into the open. A few have to be coaxed, a few have to be shamed into telling the truth, but there are others who have added their testimony to their own great achievements, and have heartened the little people everywhere in the world by their bold stand for the truth which they found in communication with the Spirit World. They found intelligent beings – some of them with characters of a nobility seldom found on earth, and they have also found their own 'dead' still living across the gulf which separates the other world from this.

Long-held opinions are the hardest to break down. Some men and women turn their faces from the light of this knowledge rather than face the small inconvenience resulting from championship of truth. Theories cannot stand in the face of facts which contradict them, even though the theories are ancient and are supported by eminent theorists of past ages. There is no argument better than a fact, and that is why you cannot shake the conviction of a man or woman who has once beheld the face of the one who loves and lives in the world beyond, or who has heard the voice, or who has felt the touch of the hand that gives confidence in times of stress.

There are the exceptional cases of men and women who have not sought personal evidence, but have investigated because they held that, if so great a truth could be demonstrated, then they ought to know so that they might bear witness to it in the world. Their number grows, but they will always be the exceptions. Always the mainstream of inquirers brought to the séance room and the Spiritualist home circle is composed of those who have 'lost' someone and seek consolation. It is the exception that they go away empty, for few there are who cannot be satisfied that the basic truth is simple to demonstrate. But the effects are tremendous, for once you prove that there is a life beyond the grave your own life must change, because your whole outlook changes. You change from the viewpoint of one who does not know to that of one who does, and it then is a matter for the individual soul to settle with himself how much he will contribute to the world that must arise one day as a result of all this evidence. No longer can you remain the same; no longer can you remain indifferent to the great questions of fear and poverty and insecurity.

No longer can a man say 'it is not my business', for he becomes responsible to the knowledge that first banished his fear that all human endeavour was in vain and that the grave swallowed his noblest aspirations as well as his body. The truth does not end with its acceptance. It works as a leaven and never can you say that you are the same and that it merely proves that you live after death. If, as we claim, this great beneficent work was set in hand because an inferior kind of human was dying into the next stage of existence, then we are bound automatically to lend our aid to the task of reform. For the kind of men and women who make the best citizens of the next world make the very best kind in this. There the only passport to progress is worth, service and the loving heart. The same qualities in this world, manifested by a large minority, would change the old order with a speed that would surprise even the most hardened.

This simple exposition may seem too simple to be true, but if you accept the first facts, you cannot escape the last. It is a great adventure when you begin your inquiry into Spiritualism, one not lightly to be undertaken. No matter what the opposition says, we are dangerous – dangerous to ignorance, intolerance, privilege, and the arrogance and aggressiveness of a purely material order of life, or even to a so-called religious order of life that denies the basic teachings of those who stood at the head of all religions when, in their purity, they were first given into the minds and hands of men.

And it induces a feeling of humility when you recall that the first step may be a Spirit drawing of the kind shown to you already a score of times.

Now all these incidents proving Survival which I have reported briefly are part of a series, and this one is as striking as any in this book. As befits a soldier, when General Sir H.

Godfrey-Morgan, V.C. appeared he showed himself so clearly that two other people in addition to the medium saw him. The General appeared so that he could be identified for his niece in whose upbringing he had been greatly concerned. The normal photograph shows how clearly the artist saw him, and how well he drew him.

5

Pioneer of Cremation

That personality developed in the mill-race of this life survives even the fires of cremation is shown in this case of the remarkable drawing of Dr. William Price. He was a pioneer – the 'inventor' of cremation in this country. It happened this way. Price's infant son 'died' and his body was burned by him in 1884. Of course there was an outcry. It could not be expected that at Llantrisant, in Wales, so revolutionary a change would go unchallenged. It was challenged, but in the end the judicial decision was that Price had done no wrong and that cremation was legal. It seems a great deal of fuss for so simple and sanitary a measure, but that is how progress is made. From the simple to the sublime is but a step, but it is hard to get human beings to take the first step.

Having established himself as a pioneer in cremation, Price lived out his full and beneficent life. Since personality must survive, he retained his interest in healing, and in time sought for a medium through whom he could work. That is how it is done. First the desire to serve, then the search for the instrument, then the training, the mission begins – and the battle opens. The medium was found. That is not the difficulty. The guides always know what they want to do, but since they must have co-operators, they then have to convince and persuade their instruments that they are what they say they are.

The medium in this case was Mrs. May Bird who, as most mediums do, doubted when first told she had psychic powers capable of development. Her work was to be healing. Her first case was not simple; a matter of cancer. She did not seek the patient. The patient sought her. Mrs. Bird went to a Spiritualist meeting at Woolwich. A woman, a stranger, begged her to give healing, "But I have never done any healing," Mrs. Bird answered.

Two years before this Mrs. Bird was told she could become a healer, but had not bothered about it. Yet this stranger insisted, and Mrs. Bird agreed to try. The patient called at her house, and when the door was opened, another walked in with her. It was Dr. William Price. He had come to take up his healing again, this time with a medium as co-operator. Mrs. Bird had the satisfaction of knowing that while the Spirit controlled her body, she remained conscious, and was a fascinated spectator of the treatment. She even heard the 'dead' man using her voice say that the patient would be healed in seventeen weeks. It was so. At the end of that time the growth disintegrated and disappeared. That was in 1917. The facts were reported in 1938, and the patient was still alive then.

Fascinating as that is, it is merely the background to the drawing which Leah did of this pioneer and healer. Mrs. Bird did not at first know who her guide was, but then he was described by other mediums. She made a trip to Wales especially to check the information, and found that the details remembered by people there corroborated what mediums told her. So far the doctor's identity seems to have been established, but it appears also that he was not satisfied, and wanted to have his portrait done. So he impressed Leah with that desire. Two portraits were done, the second one with the doctor wearing his long hair in two plaits, one behind each shoulder. This picture was finished, but Leah said nothing to Mrs. Bird – or to anyone else. He was so justifiably proud of the work that he sent it to the Royal Academy. But the artist was told at a séance that two selectors were preventing the drawing from being hung, and in time it was returned with a rejection slip. But before Mrs. Bird knew that her Spirit guide had been posing for his portrait in Leah's studio, Dr. Price mentioned it. When Mrs. Bird saw the drawing she was surprised, for always when the doctor showed himself to her, he wore a peculiar headdress. Final proof of the accuracy of the drawing came six months later when a Welsh paper printed an interview with a man who remembered Dr. Price and made a point of mentioning his long, plaited hair which hung over his shoulders. Always when out of doors he covered his plaits with his special headdress, which is shown in the photograph.

There is no point in a strict comparison between the drawing and this photograph, for the drawing is a work far beyond the old faded photograph. The drawing itself is full justification of the artist's claim to be called a portrayer of the living 'dead'. Dr. Price is shown as a living Spirit.

Still making the point that there are no limits to the evidence for Survival let us take the case of the Royal Flying Corps pilot who crashed in the First World War and whose body, though embalmed and prepared for shipment to Canada, still lies in a London vault. Captain Harold Bellamy Hamber, a Canadian, took off from Hendon to help another pilot who had come down in a field near Harlington, Bedfordshire, in 1917. With Hamber was a mechanic. Together they helped the stranded pilot to take off, and then tried to follow him. Just as their machine was airborne it turned sharply and crashed. The mechanic was killed outright, and Hamber 'died' in a military hospital the following day.

Twenty-one years later, Hamber's sister-in-law, Anne Webster, sat with Leah, with whom the appointment was made anonymously. In his usual rapid manner Leah said that Anne Webster's brother-in-law was present, that he had been in the R.F.C., gave his age as about thirty, the date of the fatal accident as late June 1917, and the place as being just outside London. The medium described the sensation of falling and crashing, the suddenness of the passing and the kind of injuries caused. Here are Anne Webster's words: "After giving an intensive and accurate description of Hamber's appearance and rather distinctive personality, transfiguration took place. Leah's face assumed the expression and features of my brother-in-law, and the left eye closed up and became swollen on the underlid. I was told that I was being given a key to 'unlock the door of ignorance'."

During the rest of the sitting Leah was taken 'out of his body' to Essex, where Anne Webster was visiting a friend at the time of the accident. There she had received the official telegram telling of Hamber's death. Following this the medium, still out of his physical body, was taken to Vancouver, where Hamber's only brother lives and where his son was brought up.

Then the psychic portrait was drawn, first without the pilot's helmet in which Hamber revealed himself later. Though the drawing may appear unusual, Anne Webster says: "It is really remarkable how the artist managed to add that helmet without concealing the pronounced widow's peak, and the parting of the hair just off the centre. This shows up clearly in both the photographs, and Leah described it in detail. We wanted a head without the helmet, so the medium sketched a second portrait.

"Hamber objected, and again showed himself in the pilot's helmet as though saying: "I'm a pilot." The portrait does so much more than just 'resemble' the photographs (which the artist did not see until two days after the sitting). It throws into startling relief a curious mixture of gaiety and tragedy so characteristic of my brother-in-law as I remember him during the weeks which preceded his passing into the Spirit World."

That is part of the record of a séance held in June 1938. In June 1939, Anne Webster wondered why Captain Hamber had withheld from Leah the fact that there was something unusual about the disposal of his body. During a talk with her, Leah later said he had received this information about the flyer's body – 'left too long with the undertaker'. That was first-class evidence, but the medium bettered it by saying that the coffin was on a shelf in a chapel in a cemetery about two miles from where she lived (near Regent's Park), and that it was with a number of other coffins. Hamber's unburied body, in its leaden shell, was for some time afterwards a place of pilgrimage for Canadian airmen and soldiers. All this Anne Webster confirms.

Not long after this evidence was given, Hamber's son arrived in London to stay with his aunt, Anne Webster. They had not met for about 18 months – that is, before the first psychic portrait was drawn. While her nephew was unpacking, Anne Webster noticed him pull out a leather folder containing a photograph of his mother, and one of his father. Tucked away in a corner of the folder was a very small snapshot of Hamber taken in a flying helmet. That recalled the incident in Leah's studio when he added the helmet at the 'dead' flier's request. Up to the moment of seeing the snapshot, Anne Webster had not seen a picture of her brother-in-law wearing a flying helmet. Then she compared the shape of this helmet in the snapshot with that drawn by Leah, and concluded there was a striking resemblance. The helmet is not the kind that airmen wear nowadays.

There is no question in that account of proved Survival that there are all the elements of intelligence, persistence, foresight, and a touch of the dramatic. It requires considerable patience, even for a 'dead' man to wait twenty-one years to prove himself, and then to wait a further year to add further evidence to something already proved.

I report now that when Anne Webster wrote of the first séance she asked that anyone who knew anything of the accident should write to her. Apparently no one did, but her vigorous brother-in-law made his own convincing testimony in his own way.

6

Evidence at Drury Lane Theatre

A strong personal attraction which she could not explain drew Mrs.W. Wade, of Surbiton, to one of the actors, F.C. Cowley Wright, in the cast of 'Decameron Nights', at Drury Lane Theatre. The attraction began a friendship not realised on earth. Mrs. Wade had not seen Cowley Wright before she entered the theatre. But she felt she knew him. It was not the acting that impressed, but the man. She made up her mind to visit the theatre again to solve the problem, but thought it could wait till she returned from a visit abroad.

While walking in the street after this decision, she heard an unfamiliar voice say: "What if he dies before you come back?" Mrs. Wade turned round to see who was talking, but saw no one. She thought at first it was strange for the twentieth century, and then, woman-like, she decided she would not be dictated to by anyone, especially by someone who had a voice but hid himself. The voice persisted, saying: "This is your last chance." Yet Mrs. Wade ignored the invisible speaker and did not go to a second performance of 'Decameron Nights'. The mysterious voice was right, for while she was abroad, Cowley Wright 'died' after being ill for only two or three days.

For years afterwards she could not rid herself of the feeling that Cowley Wright wanted her to do something. She started an inquiry into Spiritualism, and at one circle the medium gave a perfect description of Cowley Wright and spoke of his portrait, which at that time Mrs. Wade kept on her mantelpiece. Then she began to realise there was 'something' in Spiritualism. She went to many séances, and always Cowley Wright was described. Then mediums told her that the 'dead' actor would write through her hand. She developed the faculty of automatic writing, and the actor who had drawn her attention gave point after point to prove his identity until she was satisfied.

Later the gift of clear-hearing, or clairaudience, developed and the actor gave the name of a friend who had been on the stage with him, and asked Mrs. Wade to deliver a personal message. This message was of great help to the 'dead' actor's friend in a time of crisis.

Mrs. Wade wanted a permanent record of her guide's personality, and asked him whether he would co-operate if she went to see Leah. He did, for as soon as the sitting began Leah mentioned a number of points which proved to Mrs. Wade that her Spirit friend was present. Then the artist said: "Eight, ten and fifteen years." Leah asked Mrs. Wade what that meant and she explained: fifteen years since she saw Cowley Wright's performance in the theatre; ten years since she received her first Spirit message from him; eight years since she began to receive automatic writing from him.

To indicate his profession the actor showed press cuttings, gave his age correctly at the time of his 'death' as thirty-three, and a rough sketch was made in her own home Mrs. Wade told her guide that, though she was delighted with the sketch, she would like further proof of his identity, and asked him to show himself in the turban he wore at Drury Lane.

Cowley Wright agreed, and at the next séance kept his word. Leah said: "Now I see him putting on a turban. He is an actor. I see him on the stage. It is a play that has music – something like 'Chu Chin Chow', but not that play. Now he takes me down the Strand... now up Aldwych...now we are at Drury Lane Theatre... he takes me on the stage...the play is 'Decameron Nights'." Cowley Wright asked Mrs. Wade to give the excellent portrait of him all the publicity she could in the hope that it would reach people who knew him.

That is how one medium met her guide. Here is how another guide, a monk, Brother Peter, posed for his portrait to the satisfaction of his medium, Harold Sharp, who was a monk until he found that he had no vocation, and left the monastery. The portrait has the atmosphere of the monkish life, and even if you make a mask to hide the shoulders and the robe, there is still the face of a monk. The resignation is in the eyes, but there is also the kindliness of one who has done with the stress of this life, but has not done with the world.

This drawing was done in the dark while Sharp was entranced, and as Leah finished his work, he asked his Spirit caller: "Is that right?" The guide answered: "It is perfect, except for the mouth. You have mistaken my medium's mouth, with its false teeth, for mine. I will try to show myself more clearly." The medium was then transfigured and in the dark altered the mouth, the guide remarking at the end that it matched his own mouth better and made him look older than the medium – which he was at the time of his passing.

Now here is a point showing how carefully the guides work and how well they work together to make themselves and their mission clear. When Sharp was told first about Brother Peter, he confused him with a monk of that name whom he knew in the monastery in which he had served. Then Uvani, the guide of Eileen Garrett, mentioned Brother Peter. Then Arthur Ford, a famous American medium, told Sharp that he had been in a monastery, and made a forecast of his psychic work. Later Brother Peter said he was not the monk of that name whom his medium knew in the monastery, but had lived mostly in Vienna where his father was a member of the Imperial Guard. But he had served some time in England, saying he was in Camberwell, south-east London, but that public opinion was so strong against Roman Catholics in that day that he and other monks had to wear ordinary clothing.

About this extraordinary drawing Leah tells a good story against himself and his story shows how great is the force at work from the Other Side. When Leah first saw Brother Peter's portrait in *Psychic News*, he thought it so striking that he cut it out and put it on his mantelshelf. He did that so quickly that he did not read the caption or the story. Then he called up a friend and said he was so impressed with the drawing that he realised that, at last, there was another artist who could draw the 'dead'. So his friend went out, bought a copy of *Psychic News* and then telephoned to say that she appreciated the joke, but if Leah would read the story he would see that he was impressed with something he had done himself! Leah went out for another paper, and when he read the story he could not believe it. He had no recollection of the drawing or the story, although he had supplied the facts. Now I know Leah, and while normally he has a tenacious memory, this does not always apply to his psychic work. He still maintains that when he first looked at that portrait of Brother Peter, he thought it was the work of another artist. He did not at that time recall doing it.

This is the nine-second psychic drawing of Mr. Burgess of Norwich.

Photograph of Mr. Burgess, for comparison (see page 23).

From the Spirit World came this woman to pose for her portrait with the artist who clairvoyantly saw her passing. She was Ethel Gibbon's mother (see page 26).

This photograph was taken on her 102nd birthday. But she does not look it, although one of her sons-in-law said she had 'lived mostly in the Spirit World' before passing.

Monocle in left eye and long cigarette-holder were shown by Mrs. Gibbon's second husband to give the artist details of his identity (see page 25).

A photograph of Alfred Hugh Gibson M.D. for comparison with the spirit drawing (left) showing his habitual monocle – but the artist never sees a photograph until the psychic drawing is done.

The first husband of Mrs. Gibbon, Leah's psychic drawing. The moustache is highly evidential.

Normal photograph of Mrs. Gibbon's first husband showing the evidential moustache (see page 26).

Miss F.V. Gregory went to see Leah and got this psychic drawing of her mother. As the medium foretold, it took five years to find the normal photograph – shown alongside.

This second psychic portrait was drawn in one minute, showing Mrs. Gregory at 72. Her daughter had the normal photograph which is printed for comparison (see page 31).

A Spirit caricature – Thomas N. Tunbridge shows himself with his cigar and the normal photograph, smiling, still shows a cigar.

Tunbridge poses again, seriously this time, showing his carefully-kept moustache. Photograph on the right for comparison (see page 32).

The first picture is a psychic drawing of a man who decided, as his wife lay dying in the next room, that life was not worth living. The second picture is a normal photograph for comparison (see page 33).

This is how he looked 50 years before he passed. His daughter corroborated statements made by the medium, and found a prophecy about the second photograph (extreme right) came true to complete the evidence.

The first psychic drawing (left) is of a Persian who 'died' near Baghdad. Normal photograph (centre) shows the resemblance. The second psychic drawing shows him wearing an ice bandage during his last illness (see page 33).

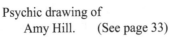

Psychic drawing of   Photograph of
Amy Hill.   (See page 33)   Amy Hill.

The first picture is a Spirit drawing of the man in the middle. The third picture is also a psychic drawing when he posed in his top hat to show how well dressed he was when he went to work (see page 34).

Psychic drawing of the
Rev. G. Gibson Gunn.

Photograph of Rev.
Gunn (see page 34).

Psychic drawing of
John Millard.

Photograph of John
Millard (see page 35).

Psychic drawing of the
'stranger'.

Photograph of the
'stranger'(see page 35).

Head of a pioneer – Leah's brilliant
psychic drawing of Dr. William Price,
pioneer of cremation (see page 40).

Dr. William Price, of Llantrisant, burned the body of his infant son who had 'died'. A legal battle followed, and the judge gave the doctor the verdict. So cremation became legal in Britain. The photograph printed above shows Dr. Price holding a torch. He is wearing a headdress he designed for himself and which he always wore out of doors to cover his long plaits (see page 42).

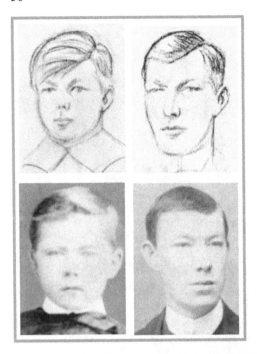

Seven times Percy George Stocker posed for Frank Leah for the seven Spirit drawings shown on these two pages. Stocker's family produced these seven photographs, some faded with age, for comparison (see pages 28-29).

Psychic drawing and photograph of
Mrs. Ramsay (see page 36).

Psychic drawing and photograph of
Brig. Gen. Sir H. Godfrey-Morgan
(see page 38).

This 'flying helmet' snapshot (above)
of Capt. Hamber who 'died' in 1917
came to light ten months after the
highly evidential psychic drawing
(right) was drawn. Hamber's son
brought the snapshot from Paris to
London (see page 43).

Photograph of Cowley Wright in his turban, as he appeared in 'Decameron Nights' at Drury Lane Theatre.

Leah's psychic drawing of Cowley Wright showing the turban and his straight back hair.

This photograph of Cowley Wright shows the strong resemblance to the turbanned psychic portrait (see page 45).

'The Spirit of the monastery' — Brother Peter, an Austrian monk, Spirit guide of Harold Sharp, who himself was a monk until he felt he had no vocation. Sharp knew a Brother Peter in the monastery, but his own guide cleared up the confusion and established his own identity (see page 47).

Farmer Knowles, a rough
psychic sketch.

A normal photograph of
Farmer Knowles (see page 89).

There is no normal photograph of Dr. Letari, Spirit guide of Lilley, the healer, for comparison. But the doctor said when shown this drawing that if he had seen it as his own reflection in a mirror, he would have been well pleased at the spectacle (see page 85).

Psychic drawing of Fred Edouin.

For only a few weeks in his life Fred Edouin, direct voice medium, wore a moustache. So that is how he showed himself to the artist who knew him, but had never seen him with a moustache. Mrs. Edouin had seen a 'moustache' photograph but could not trace it. The photograph left is for comparison with the psychic drawing above (see page 81).

This photograph of the father of Fred Edouin, the medium, is printed here for comparison with Frank Leah's psychic portrait below. Three people at the seance at which the portrait was done saw the 'dead' man in addition to the artist, who insisted on their signing the portrait before he would look at a photograph (see page 83).

Psychic drawing of Fred Edouin's father.

Coventry Patmore, the 19th century poet, inspires his grandson, Deighton Patmore, the healer. This photograph (left) is printed for comparison with Frank Leah's psychic portrait reproduced below which was drawn in two and a half minutes. There is a strong resemblance – but Leah had not seen the photograph: he saw only the Spirit form of the poet (see page 88).

"'Now I have lasting proof of Survival; no one can ever take this from me," says Mrs. F. D.Thain of this psychic portrait (above). When she visited the artist to keep her appointment her 'dead' husband's picture was ready completed. The snapshot, printed for comparison, was taken on their wedding day. It is the only photograph of him that Mrs. Thain possesses (see page 90).

Leah's psychic portrait of John Teverson (see page 92).

Photograph of John Teverson for comparison.

Though the artist did a good likeness of Rhoda Ring in one minute, he could not resist doing this one (above) in her mother's presence. She considers it an even better likeness. The snapshot on the left is for comparison (see page 93).

This striking and, say the parents, characteristic drawing of six-year-old Shirley Ann Woods was drawn by Frank Leah after he had described her accurately to her mother on the telephone. Only after they saw the psychic drawing did they show the artist this small snapshot. Mrs. Woods has no doubt that the psychic portrait is her child (see page 96).

Frankness is one of Frank Leah's characteristics. He proved to G.R. Blaylock of Burnley, Lancs that his 'dead' wife was present by telling him she was urging the artist to make a cup of tea. Not only did the medium draw a sketch of Mrs. Blaylock but gave her husband evidence which he said was correct. The snapshot shows Mrs. Blaylock when she was ten years younger (see page 96).

"It almost speaks," says Miss Wagstaff, of Hemingford Road, Cheam, Surrey, of this drawing of her brother, J.W.D. Wagstaff. Miss Wagstaff compared Leah's portrait with two snapshots of her brother, and says of them: "Neither contains anything like the detail shown

in Mr. Leah's portrait." For comparison a snapshot is shown (see page 97).

The artist drew this portrait of the spirit of a young officer whose father says it is 'indisputable'. It was finished in the father's presence (see page 98).

One of the few photographs in this book without a name – at the father's request. So we call him 'A.P.'. Even without a name the evidence is there.

This psychic drawing was promised by a mother to her daughter, from the Other Side. The mother said she wished to be seen as she really was. She did - even to the bun in her hair (see page 99).

Mrs. Clarke, of Bexley, Kent, was grieved always when she saw this photo of her mother, showing a face drawn with pain. Although Leah had not seen this picture he described the collar she wore.

Mediums like to have evidence as well as other people. When Mrs. Louie Hill stopped her jam-making to telephone Leah for an appointment she had in mind a portrait of her spirit guide. First she got a psychic portrait of her 'dead' father, and then one of her guide who brought him to the artist's studio. On the right is a photograph of her father which she had forgotten about (see page 101).

Robert Hollington 'died' fighting the Japanese in Burma. His mother hoped he was still on earth.

Leah had never seen a photograph of Robert Hollington when he drew this psychic portrait (see page 103).

John Hollington 'died' in a reconnaissance flight over Germany on September 30 1939.

This is how the young airman showed himself, still full of life, to the artist (see page 104).

72

This psychic drawing shows that Mrs. Arthur Smith of Wolverhampton, dressed her hair in this style. But her husband denied it was brought so low down (see page 106).

When Arthur Smith compared this normal photograph with the psychic portrait, he admitted the medium was right and that his wife wore her hair low on her forehead.

"After I have left this sphere I will try to come to you," wrote this musician – and this is how he appeared to the artist (see page 108).

A normal photograph of Mr. H. Wharton-Wells – a former organist of Putney Parish Church – for comparison with the psychic drawing.

Above: Spirit drawing of an officer who became a Spirit guide.

Below is a normal photograph of this officer who passed over in the South African War (see page 111).

Psychic drawing of a parson who disliked his clerical collar (note the clerical collar, bottom right).

Dr. Margaret Vivian's father. Photograph for comparison (see page 111).

Vivid Spirit portrait of Dr. Vivian's mother (see page 111).

And here is a normal photograph of her.

'A wonderful work'
is how the St. Nazaire
hero's father describes
his psychic drawing.

For comparison here is a photograph of
the young lieutenant who said he hoped
he was dying to help make the world a
better place.   (see page 112)

William Hope of Crewe, whom everybody called 'Billy', proved the survival of thousands with his psychic photographs. He proved his own survival in the most dramatic circumstances, transfiguring the face of a friend so that the artist could see his face for the striking psychic portrait which was then executed in seven minutes.

Leah had never met Hope; had not even seen a picture of the man who had so often photographed the 'dead' (see page 114).

Normal picture of Hope.

Left: Psychic drawing of
Archdeacon Richardson
of Ontario, Canada.

Below: Normal photograph
later sent from America by
his son (see page 115).

Left: Bust modelled in two
hours, based on Leah's
psychic portrait (see page
116).

7

Medium Proves His Survival

If you are a beginner you have been gradually led to the view that there is more in this Spiritualism than just saying something at a séance which will indicate or even prove to someone who knows you that you still live. Little by little, I have tried to lead you to an expanding view of order, purpose and wisdom in the work of that vast army of Spirits who stand behind humanity serving, albeit unknown to most of those they seek to help. Therefore, having persevered so far, here is a case of Spirit identity proved through a series of facts that are woven into a complex but complete pattern. Here is the revelation of personality seeking to impress itself – and succeeding.

The Spirit whose portrait, or portraits, are the subject of this account was in this life a well-known medium – Fred Edouin. The facts are attested partly by his wife, Irene Edouin, also a medium, and by Leah. There was this difficulty to overcome, that Leah knew Edouin slightly before he passed. Therefore, it was harder to draw an evidential portrait.

Leah did try to do a drawing from memory, but trained in observation though he is, he could not recapture the features of the man he knew. The account of the triumph of the artist and the 'dead' medium is best told by Mrs. Edouin. Five or six times she tried to write the story, but went to bed still displeased with her work. Early next morning she felt a touch on her shoulder, and her husband – who was a journalist – asked her to rise and try again. Without any change this is the story which she typed straight off after that request:

"I should like to put on record another experience I have had concerning the efforts of my husband, Fred Edouin, to prove the truth of communication, this time through the mediumship of Mr. Frank Leah. Last year [this was written in 1939] Mr. Leah attended a voice circle at which Mr. Edouin was the medium, and expressed a wish to draw a portrait of one of the controls, named Jack. I think that during the circle Jack himself said he would very much like it done. Mr. Leah kindly arranged to come to a sitting with Mr. Edouin, and the result was a splendid portrait, and considered an excellent likeness by many who had seen Jack clairvoyantly. After that my husband was very anxious that Mr. Leah should try and obtain one of his principal control, Dr. Hylton, and finally a sitting with Mr. Leah was arranged for October 10. This, however, had to be postponed, through Mr. Edouin's being called away on business.

"Since that time we had not seen Mr. Leah or been in contact with him. After my husband's passing I was requested by many to put on record our voice circle experiences, and when I started to gather the material, I realised it would be incomplete without a portrait of Dr. Hylton.

"I was in Italy at the time and I intended, on my return home again, to approach Mr. Leah with a view to a sitting in hopes of being able to obtain the picture. However, there was nothing of this in my mind when, on the morning of March 6, I sat down to send a few remaining postcards to friends. We left Genoa on the fourth, and were approaching Algiers. I had finished, as I thought, when I became acutely aware of my husband's presence.

"I knew there was something or somebody he was trying to remind me of, but I could not make out what or who. I picked up my address book, which opened for no apparent reason at the letter 'L'. I looked through the names, but nothing impressed me. I went slowly through the book, but still did not understand.

I felt him grow a little impatient. At this point, a fellow-passenger came up and we talked for a few minutes. As she turned to go, she knocked some of my papers off my desk, the address book among them. As we bent to pick them up there lay the address book again at the letter 'L'.

"Then from the rest seemed to stand out the name, 'Frank Leah'. In a flash I realised he was reminding me of Dr. Hylton's portrait which I should require for the book. I wrote to Mr. Leah straight away, and explained the circumstances, and said I would ring him on my return. When I arrived home Mr. Leah rang me up and said that he had had a very remarkable experience regarding my husband. Whilst quietly concentrating on the previous Monday morning, Mr. Edouin had literally barged into his room, full of energy and life. Mr. Leah was out of London at the time of my husband's passing, and, remembering that he had not written, said: "All right, I will write to your wife." He got the reply: "Don't trouble, she is writing to you." Now on comparing notes we found I must have been writing about that time.

"I spoke about Dr. Hylton's portrait, and Mr. Leah said: 'Certainly, but there is something else he wants me to do. He comes to me frequently, each time showing himself as a much younger man, in uniform, with a moustache, somewhere in the twenties.' However, we proceeded to have the sitting for Dr. Hylton's portrait and had amazing results, the first sitting being entirely successful, but through it all Mr. Edouin continued to show himself in uniform, and Mr. Leah said he knew he had to do a portrait of him at that time. It is interesting here to explain that when Mr. Edouin had a photograph taken in uniform, with a moustache, it was a year before I even knew him, and only once had I seen this photograph, shown to me by a sister who had kept it as a joke. He looked so entirely different with a moustache, and he grew it for only a few weeks.

"Hoping I could get this photograph from her, Mr. Leah decided to try and get the likeness, and we started sittings for that on April 1, and asked an independent sitter, Mr. G. Howell Smith, to join us. We had a good red light at the first séance, but from beginning to end raps and noises came in rapid succession from a corner of the room, and once it seemed as if there was a faint attempt at a voice. At that sitting Mr. Leah roughly outlined the head and features, but at the second sitting more interesting things began to happen. The physical phenomena ceased, but Mr. Leah underwent a series of transfigurations. His body and shoulders expanded. The head began to alter in shape, and the high forehead was particularly noticeable.

"At this stage Mr. Leah found slight difficulty in deciding which side the hair was parted on. This was very interesting, as my husband was in the habit of parting it in different places, seldom using exactly the same parting, and frequently changing the style; this he believed helped to prevent thinness, and as baldness ran in the family he was anxious to avoid it at an early age. However after changing it several times, Mr Leah decided on the left, which was correct according to other photographs taken about that time. Mr. Leah at this sitting made two rough sketches which showed amazing likenesses to pictures taken at that age, but he was not satisfied.

"The next sitting took place the following Saturday, and produced evidence in matters that Mr. Leah could not possibly have known. He complained at once that he had a severe pain in the left eye, and he found difficulty in keeping it open. At all times when Mr. Edouin was not well, his left eye would half close. During the last few months of his earthly life it had grown extremely painful. The transfiguration was always very apparent, and there was pain in the body which seemed to have distended Mr. Leah to a state of acute discomfort.

"At this sitting the drawing of the nose and mouth gave difficulty, which again was very good evidence. The shape of my husband's mouth was a little different in later years owing to all his top teeth being removed, the artificial ones giving a fuller line to the mouth. A motor accident caused a broken nose which quite altered the line when in profile, one side being quite aquiline and the other side a 'pug nose'.

"One thing I have noticed, but had not mentioned, was that the moustache was not quite correct. At this third sitting Mr. Leah suddenly said, rubbing his own lip: "The moustache is all wrong." In about five seconds he corrected it.

"Mr. Leah still wished for one more sitting, and I was very glad to have the opportunity of having a further one of the experiences which had all been outstanding. During those sittings Mr. Leah passed through every change of feature that I know of, and can prove, during twenty years. At times it was as if a mask was held up in front of his face; and the psychic power was such that neither Mr. Howell Smith nor I could move. At the last sitting Mr. Leah was once again removed   from our sight and, built up in front of him, through the mask condition, I saw quite distinctly my husband as he was when I first met him. There is no photograph, as far as I know, in existence like it.

"At the time of writing, although I have inquired from all his relatives, I cannot obtain the picture he tried so hard to portray. The portrait [Leah's psychic portrait] as it was when finished, is outstanding. I consider it a remarkable likeness, a triumph for the proof of Spirit return and of the reality of Mr. Leah's mediumship."

Like many good stories this one has a sequel. Shortly after these facts were reported, Leah said that a week before his birthday – which was on April 27 – he saw Edouin in his flat with his father, of whom he had not heard before. He understood they had come to have a portrait done, so he arranged a sitting with Mrs. Edouin. Three of the sitters saw Edouin's father in addition to the artist. When the portrait was completed the artist insisted on the sitters signing it – even before he would look at a photograph.

It is a splendid likeness. A few days later, on the morning of his birthday, Leah again saw Edouin in his flat, and the Spirit worried him until he rang up Mrs. Edouin and repeated the message he gave. He was passing on the message saying that the 'dead' man was very joyful and sent his best wishes, for there was something special about the day. "Before you speak," said Leah, "I should say it is my birthday to-day and the message might have something to do with that."

Mrs. Edouin replied that it was also her birthday that day, and also her daughter-in-law's birthday. Fred Edouin always took the family out to dinner and the theatre on that day, which was a family festival. Later that afternoon Leah was talking to another Spirit guide who conveyed Edouin's thanks for talking to his wife that morning, as it had given her a great deal of happiness. Then the Spirit spoke of a 'funny' parcel which had come, or was to come, by post. She was going to say more, but Edouin stopped her.

Next morning the postman delivered the 'funny' parcel. It was a birthday present, a cigarette box, sent by Mrs. Edouin. She stressed that it was a present from her husband, and not from her. She said also that at about the time when Leah was talking to the Spirit who mentioned Edouin and the 'funny' parcel, her husband had come to her and insisted that she should go out and buy the present for Leah.

We may forget. The 'dead' never do.

Still the Spirit guides press forward to prove themselves. Dr. Letari is the guide of W. H. Lilley, the famous psychic healer, who knew very well how he looked before he spoke to Leah for the first time on the telephone. A mutual friend introduced them, and on the telephone Leah gave Lilley a detailed description of his guide, so accurate that the healer said: "No one has ever given me such an accurate description of my guide." All the facts tallied with what Lilley already knew – that the 'dead' doctor was exceptionally short, about five feet one, and that his eyes had an intense look. But one point mentioned by Leah was not admitted by Lilley – that the Hindu doctor wore a moustache. Then a meeting was arranged, and with his medium entranced Letari told Leah that he was right about the moustache. He wore it from 1910 to 1912, when he was in England studying surgery. Letari also confirmed all Leah's earlier statements, including the fact that he passed at Peshawar, in the Khyber Pass, India.

Then Leah went on with the portrait, and when the medium came out of trance he exclaimed: "That's the doctor." Well, as you see, the portrait was done with the disputed moustache, and when the finishing touches were added later, the doctor again entranced his medium and with the unfailing courtesy of the 'dead' said: "If you will give me permission, I would consider it a privilege to sign it." Holding the pencil as though it were a pointer, he wrote his name in the symbols of his race, indicating both his profession and status. He added that if he had seen the portrait as his own reflection in a mirror, he would have been pleased with the spectacle.

Thousands of people have been treated by Lilley, who is the instrument for a group of doctors who have not lost their interest because they have lost their bodies. Instead they co-operate and add to the knowledge they gained here the greater knowledge that exists in the Spirit World where a man or woman naturally interested in healing and trained in any technique must find greater opportunities for serving.

You can well imagine that when a patient sees the portrait of a doctor who though 'dead' still lives and heals, he is a little encouraged to go on, for much as we all say we have faith when we are in the flush of enthusiasm born of the acquisition of a few new facts, we all like to be encouraged – especially by a 'sign'. There is little better to reassure you than to see the face of the one you trust, although it may be only a few lines on a piece of paper. That is how we are made, and that is why the Spirit guides go to endless trouble to see that we have the evidence we need to lighten us on our way in this world.

It is a truism to experienced Spiritualists that there is more evidence than there are people ready to receive it, and also that there are more guides trained and waiting to co-operate with us here than there are mediums or instruments. That is part of the explanation why many mediums have to be taken a long way round sometimes to come to their real work in life though, of course, most do not see at the time of their experiencing difficulties that it is part of a plan.

8

Coventry Patmore Returns

This is an illustration of what I mean. J. Deighton Patmore, grandson of the nineteenth century poet, Coventry Patmore, was a very wealthy man. Now he is a healer, well known for the use of curative colour lamps which he invented. The development of Patmore's healing and the proof of his grandfather's Survival are bound up together.

That is where the Leah portrait is valuable. For days the 'dead' poet appeared to the artist, urging him to visit his grandson. In the end Leah telephoned J. Deighton Patmore saying he must see him. All the artist asked for when he arrived was a small table – and silence. He was tense, and stood for a while looking at the carpet, his head following an imaginary line which, by habit, Deighton Patmore always walked when dealing with a problem or when dictating. Leah later explained that he saw Coventry Patmore pacing this line with his hands behind his back, a favourite mannerism when concerned over anything. The grandson had unconsciously copied the habit.

Then Leah, in two-and-a-half minutes, did the portrait of the poet who had asked him to visit his grandson. The drawing is a striking resemblance of the photograph with which it is compared – but which he did not see until his work was done. The portrait is unlike the Sargent painting in the National Gallery.

Deighton Patmore knows that his grandfather is inspiring him in his work, and he is not interested in the reproach – like the one sent him in a newspaper cutting – that the poet's grave is neglected. He knows that the poet, whose hobby here was colour, is still alive, and is working with him to heal.

Deighton Patmore's healing began after a series of heavy financial losses had reduced him to poverty. Moreover, he had been ill. As always when the crisis is reached, the solution appears. When Patmore was at his lowest he became aware of a force in his fingers. He did not understand it, but was impressed with the idea that he could heal people. He found that by massage he could, in a few minutes, drive pain away. His first experiments with colour-wave lamps were made for decorative purposes. Then he found that they, too, had a healing power.

One of his first patients was a woman who had been deaf for about twelve years. Doctors said she was incurable. As Deighton Patmore was treating her, noises which she had heard in her head for years stopped. Then she heard normally, and became so excited that the healer turned on a colour lamp to soothe her. Patmore and his secretary, who knew nothing of Spiritualism, were surprised when the patient was entranced, and a deep masculine voice spoke through her telling him to continue his work in which he would be helped from the Other Side. Though the identity of the voice was not given, the similarity to the healer's way of speaking suggested that it was a relative. First he thought it was his father. Then he realised it was his grandfather, Coventry Patmore. That started the healer's inquiry into Spiritualism, and soon he was convinced that his power came from Spirit helpers. Several mediums described the 'dead' poet to him, and one said Deighton Patmore would write a book and publish it. He laughed at that, but his book *Mirrors of Life* was published.

So you see, it is all bound up together. There are no watertight compartments in the case of Survival. One faculty shades off into another, one kind of evidence begets another, and one medium's work is woven into another's, and the great and beneficent truth is spread for all mankind to share.

That is the story of a poet. Now here is a story of a peasant, or rather a cattle-dealer. Stephen Knowles, of Bridgwater, Somerset, wrote this testimony to the value of the psychic artist's work: "Frank Leah did not know me from Adam, yet within five minutes he drew my father who passed in 1915." Knowles heard Leah give a lantern lecture on his work, and asked for a sitting. The result was the portrait, and says Knowles:

"When I showed Leah's sketch to my father's favourite son, who knows nothing about Spiritualism and asked him: 'Does this remind you of anybody?' my brother replied: 'Why, it's Dad.'

"At another séance Leah made an excellent sketch of my 'dead' mother, but unfortunately there is no picture to show for comparison. The medium described the two-storeyed farmhouse in which my parents lived, and said he could see cattle. My father was a cattle-dealer. Leah accurately described my mother's last condition and added: "I see a Georgian dragon brooch." My mother wore as a brooch a mounted five-shilling piece which shows St. George and the dragon. The medium also told me the date of her passing, 1894, and added that she was forty-four and 'died' after a childbirth. My mother passed on ten days after I was born."

You cannot imagine facts like these; you cannot imagine a cattle-dealer living in a two-storeyed farmhouse. The first kind of man you would expect to live in a farmhouse would be a farmer. And then you have to guess how he looks, and so on and on until, if you are reasonable and are prepared to face facts, you have to admit that the case for Spiritualism is proved even on the cases of Survival in this book. It makes no difference where you choose – all the facts are there. It depends on us what we do with them.

Of course, if you feel like it, you can still shrug your shoulders and say:

"Well, what of it?" There is an answer even to that attitude, as there is for all reactions to facts. Here is the reply to the doubting Thomases who have to be convinced against their wall of obstinacy. It is in the words of Mrs. F. D. Thain, of

Normanshire Drive, Chingford, East London, who said after she saw Leah's portrait of her 'dead' husband: "When gazing at the portrait I felt as though I was seeing my husband at last after a long separation. The temptation to take the portrait in my arms was almost irresistible, so realistic was it. Can anyone dare say after such evidence from a stranger that after death we are less than nothing? Imagination or a flair for fiction could never in a million years have given such over-whelming and accurate evidence."

Mrs. Thain heard first of Leah's mediumship through *Psychic News*, the agency which has brought comfort to tens of thousands. She was a stranger to the medium when they met. She believed that her husband was safe and happy, but she said: "I desperately needed some worldly proof of his continued existence. Now I have a lasting proof of his Survival. No one can ever take this from me."

As is very often the case, the first contact with Leah was by telephone, when the medium gave an accurate description of the 'dead' man. Leah said he was not a war casualty, and made this comment – for often there is reproduced in his own body the pain and conditions of passing of those who present themselves for portraits – "He had some trouble with his lungs because I can feel a terrible difficulty in breathing. His heart had been strained." Then his age was given as twenty-four. This is Mrs. Thain's opinion of that description: "So perfectly true. None could have so described him even while on earth in the flesh. My last lingering doubts disappeared."

Though the artist had no model, no photograph to go on, he had completed a sketch when Mrs.Thain called on him. This is her opinion of it: "The likeness to my husband during his last days on earth was uncanny. As I was the only one present at his so-called 'death bed' this made it sufficient proof even for the most sceptical."

Then Leah started to make alterations to the sketch because, he said, in its original state he considered it too great a reminder of pain. As he finished the changes he experienced "a terrible stab in the heart, rapid pulse, a weakness at the knees." Some days later Mrs. Thain again visited the artist, and as he was passing on some messages received from her husband, he felt the same stab in the heart. Although he was in distress he insisted on making some further adjustments to the portrait.

Is it likely that Leah, a man of sensitive temperament and wide experience, would invent a piece of play-acting to impress a woman in search of evidence that the man she loves still lives? Is it likely that he could imagine where the pain would be? Is it likely that everything is imagined or the result of collusion? All the living are not fools, neither are the 'dead' stupid. These facts are living things with which the world has to reckon. They are true; they are helpful; they drive away ignorance; they still the fears of the sorrowing heart; they give new hope where hope lay crushed; and they dry the tears of those who cannot live without the warm human companionship that is found in love.

Having proved everything we claim, we pass on to still further proof, because it never ends.

No member of the Teverson family, of Mount Park Avenue, South Croydon, Surrey, ever met Frank Leah with the exception of the younger son who called at his studio for the finished portrait of his brother, John, who passed during the typhoid outbreak at Croydon. Yet this is what the mother said: "All my relatives and friends who have seen the sketch have immediately recognised my son. One friend, herself an artist, thinks Leah could not have got a better portrait if my son had sat for him." That is high praise, but the evidence has only begun. The only time they have spoken was over the telephone about an hour after Leah received a letter from her asking for a sitting a month ahead. In that letter she also asked for a sitting for a friend, Frank Derham, a few days ahead.

Just after he received the note, Leah telephoned from his flat in west London to Mrs. Teverson in Croydon, saying that with him was a young man whom he knew was her son. He asked her to get a pencil and paper and note the clairvoyant description he then gave. Leah said the young man was tall, slim, had brown hair, parted on the left, naturally wavy, wore a Ronald Colman moustache, and had very white, well-kept teeth. Describing the young man as a boy because of his youthful appearance, Leah said he saw him smiling, and gathered that he worked in an office, was fond of sport, and was to have been married shortly. Mrs. Teverson recognised all this as a perfect description of her son who 'died' in 1937 at the age of twenty-nine. He was an accountant, and was to have been married three months from the date of his passing. His home was nearly ready.

Then Leah said he was doing a sketch of the young man. On the following Thursday, the artist telephoned again to say that the boy had shown himself once more at two o'clock in the morning, but from another angle. Again the evidential nature of Leah's work is shown by the following: Frank Derham, for whom Mrs. Teverson made an appointment by letter, kept it the day on which Leah telephoned to say that John Teverson had shown himself again. When Derham saw the sketch on the easel, he immediately recognised it from the many psychic visions he had of him, for he was then developing as a medium. But he had never met John Teverson, nor had he ever seen a photograph of him, although he was a member of the same Spiritualist circle as Mrs. Teverson. She kept all her son's photographs in a drawer. Mrs. Teverson is a Spiritualist, of course, but all the facts are there to show that neither time, nor distance, nor the fact that the artist never met a man in the flesh can prevent an excellent portrait being done so long as the psychic faculties and the artistic abilities are there.

The two pictures – the psychic portrait and the photograph – show how much the artist has captured the personality of the young man who left this life when he was about to begin it fully.

A minute is not long. But it was just long enough for Mrs. K. M. Ring, of Newbury, Berks, to hear Leah give a detailed description of her daughter and to draw a portrait of her. This happened when Mrs. Ring called on the artist on the anniversary of her 'dead' daughter's birthday. Though Leah is critical of his work, he regards this portrait as an outstanding achievement, for it is seldom that he, rapid worker though he is, does a drawing at such speed. He thinks the pace and accuracy in this case are due to the strong rapport achieved between himself and the Spirit girl. Leah said: "She was so active that I could not resist making another sketch in the presence of a responsible person." This drawing, done four days after the first – when the mother was present – he says is an even better likeness. The 'dead' girl, to show how much she is alive, impressed on her mother her desire for a third portrait, and indicated which expression she wished to have portrayed. To help the artist she showed herself in a number of poses, including a profile, which is part of the evidence, for Rhoda was always sensitive over the size of her nose, and Leah has reproduced this feature. But in the Spirit World, Rhoda has got over her sensitiveness.

When Mrs. Ring visited the artist for the second time she found the third portrait completed, but Rhoda was still active, so active, said Leah, that "not for a long time has a communicator shown herself in so many different positions or given so little trouble. It has been a grand experience. I could have done at least another two portraits of her."

But Mrs. Ring goes further, and says that the full-face portrait is a truer likeness than the photograph which is printed for comparison.

There is, as always, a little more to this account. The day before she visited Leah for the first time she wrote a birthday letter to her daughter, and left it open on her dressing-table. Then she went to have a sitting with Joseph Benjamin, the east London medium, through whom Rhoda proved herself in many ways, repeating also the contents of the birthday letter. She also promised a portrait, and a few hours later kept her promise. Later Mrs. Ring found the word 'Rhoda' written on the back of a letter in her handbag. Now she is an enthusiastic Spiritualist.

9

Child Who Came Back

That the bond between mother and child is not severed when the silver cord is broken is proved by this instance of six-year-old Shirley Ann Woods who returned to prove her Survival to her mother. Shirley Ann 'died' in 1939, though the best medical skill obtainable was lavished on her. Mrs. Woods was a Roman Catholic. Her husband, an accountant, was an agnostic. Soon after the little girl passed on he began an inquiry into Spiritualism, and at one séance was given impressive evidence in the form of messages from her. To Mrs. Woods the word of her Church was law, and the law of Rome is that Spiritualism is outlawed. Priests have written much about Spiritualism, and their verdict, by a freak of coincidence, is unanimous – against it. The editor of *Psychic News* met Mrs. Woods and told her he was surprised that a highly-intelligent woman with a twentieth-century outlook should permit priests to dictate to her and so compel her to abdicate her reason in so vital a matter. In a long argument Mrs. Woods defended her Roman Catholic point of view.

It often happens that when opponents of Spiritualism, or those who have not inquired, are firmest in their theoretical belief that it is unfounded, they are nearest to conviction. That is my experience, and in Mrs. Woods' case it was certainly true, for not long after this argument she read Arthur Findlay's book, *The Psychic Stream*, which tells of the origin and source of the Christian faith. Her husband was reading it, and Mrs. Woods was curious, so she looked into it casually at first, then read all the 1159 pages. Woman-like, she asked her husband why he had not told her about it! That was one step nearer inquiry, but really this was unorthodox, for Rome does not approve of the faithful reading dangerous books like those written by Findlay. Soon after she started her round of séances, Mrs. Woods also read the best books she could find on Spiritualism. All séances were not equally successful, but in six months enough evidence was gathered in the satchel of memory to prove that there is a life beyond the tomb and that the warm hands of a child and the clear questing eyes do not lose their brightness to cold clay.

As Mrs. Woods pursued her quest, her husband analysed all her evidence, so that the spur of enthusiasm should not speed her beyond the bounds of safe knowledge. The next step was to telephone Leah – from her home in Elstree – but the artist was engaged. So she telephoned again, at 11p.m. The artist was not told what was wanted, but he informed Mrs. Woods that she sought a portrait of her child. And he described her exactly, remarking on her 'dark, dank hair,' described her eyes, her slight figure, pale complexion, penetrating look, and then outlined her character.

By this time the mother was convinced that Leah was looking at Shirley Ann. He suggested that Mrs. Woods should call in three days, during which time he thought he could draw what he had seen. With Mrs. Woods went her three-year-old boy – who does not resemble his sister – and as soon as they arrived in the studio Leah began to draw. But the little boy was a distraction. Three days later Mrs. Woods called on the artist alone, and the portrait was completed. There is no photograph like this sketch, which the mother describes as a 'wonderful impression'. The artist was induced to draw a break in the fringe, which was a feature in the child's hair, something a mother would remember. Also Leah wished to draw a bow. This the mother could not understand until she looked at an enlargement of a snapshot, and found that the 'bow' appearance was caused by something worn by a little boy standing behind her girl.

Now her husband, who was the first to be convinced, was sceptical of this latest piece of evidence when his wife told him about it, but he promised to call for the picture. He, too, was impressed when he saw it. As so often happens with this medium, Leah was so moved by further details that he did a second portrait showing Shirley Ann's unusually penetrating eyes for one so young, the formation of her mouth, and the tilt of her head. The father was in the studio when this portrait was done without aid from any photograph or snapshot – or even the first psychic drawing. The little girl not only showed herself, but also Spirit photographs of herself. One further point that Leah could not have guessed, but which he drew – the child in both drawings is wearing a plaid frock. Later the parents produced pictures of their daughter wearing this plaid frock. The end of this story is that the little girl spoke of the Leah portrait of herself when a few days later her mother had a sitting with Estelle Roberts.

It is some distance in the human mind from agnosticism to belief, or from Roman Catholicism to belief in Survival, but it is, in fact, no further than the distance from assumption or denial to fact. For some the road is endless; to others it is a few steps.

Do you think there is any evidence in a cup of tea? Mr. G. K. Blaylock, of Leamington Avenue, Burnley, thinks so, for when he called on Frank Leah, the artist began to draw a portrait of his 'dead' wife. "She is telling me," said the artist, "to make you a cup of tea." And he stopped his drawing and made tea. Now the evidence in that cup of tea is that Blaylock is very fond of tea and his wife said she was always making it for him. It is in small things like that the greater truths are hidden, for little by little they build up until they present a picture as convincing as any drawing done by Leah.

In this instance also the evidence for Survival was clinched by a portrait of a woman whom he accurately described as determined, quick-tempered, and an animal-lover who was intolerant of those who were not. He said also that she was stockily built, about five-feet-two, and had a full set of false teeth. The husband's answer to all those points was 'correct'.

Then he left the studio to keep a business appointment, and when he returned Leah had completed a second and entirely different portrait. The artist had not yet seen a photograph of the 'dead' woman, but when the second drawing was done it was obvious that it strikingly resembled a picture taken when Mrs. Blaylock was much younger. Two further points of evidence were given. The medium felt severe pains below the knees. Mrs. Blaylock experienced these before passing. "Then," said the artist, "your wife 'died' as a result of a heart attack out of doors." The husband answered "True", and he whose evidence began with a cup of tea ended with a cup filled with the happiness that comes from reunion with the one he loves.

A psychic portrait, excelling a photograph for detailed resemblance, was drawn by Leah when Miss A.Wagstaff, of Hemingford Road, Cheam, Surrey, visited his studio after the 'death' of her brother. But before that, when she telephoned for an appointment, she was told – to her "utter amazement" she said – of her relationship to the young man whose portrait she desired, his age, and the year in which he passed. Miss Wagstaff had two snapshots of her brother, but on comparing them with the artist's work she says: "Neither contains anything like the detail shown in Mr. Leah's portraits." The first sketch was done within ten minutes of Miss Wagstaff arriving in the studio. "It almost speaks," she said, but of the second one she stated: "If possible, better than the first."

Again, here the medium experienced in some degree the pains suffered by the young man before he passed – heart pains and a gradual weakening of the voice. For the Wagstaff family there is the comfort now of two excellent portraits – and the assurance that the son lives on, as he proved, for a man who does not exist cannot very well pose for his portrait.

There is another family happier because Leah serves faithfully the light he has received. There is no name here – only the initials A.P. That is how they wish it, but the family of A.P. – also in Surrey, the same county as the Wagstaffs of Cheam, have the consolation of a likeness of a young army officer who 'died' while on leave in August, 1941. Then A.P. telephoned the artist who was unknown to him. The A.P. family knew nothing of psychic subjects. But when the father was asking Leah over the telephone for an appointment a description was given.

"I was informed," said A.P., "with faithful detail, of the passing of a near relative whose death was undoubtedly hastened by the news of the earlier major tragedy." Both men passed after an explosion. The father, A.P. added: "The sexes and ages of the two young victims, the explosion and its location, and description of two characters indirectly concerned followed." This talk lasted 40 minutes and left the father, as he said, "definitely surprised". That same evening, again on the telephone, Leah gave the father details "of a family nature, also certain facial characteristics and mannerisms which definitely established the figure described as that of our son."

Next day the father called on the artist and found a head-and-shoulders sketch of his son waiting. In the father's presence it was finished, but no details were altered. After what he described as an "unusual experiment", A.P. accepted as "indisputable throughout, and comparison of the photograph of our son, taken at the age of twenty, with the psychic sketch at twenty-three years, is sufficient proof, if such were necessary, of the greatness of Mr. Leah's work."

Both were from Surrey, but both are in the same Spirit World, and though the chances of these two young men meeting in life were remote, they both had to come to the studio of the artist-medium of whose existence they could not even have dreamt before they passed. Now, can you imagine how in two homes certainty of reunion replaces fear and the empty ache that comes from uncertainty?

"I had amazing proof of personality surviving death," wrote Mrs. Frances L. Clarke, of Blendon, Bexley, Kent, after Leah drew the portrait her mother always promised even before she 'died'. Mrs. Clarke wrote also: "It always grieved me that my only photograph of my mother was such a sad and drawn affair. She had often said since her passing that I should have one of her as she really was."

As nearly always is the case, the first contact was made by telephone, when the artist said he could see a man and a woman, but that Mrs. Clarke wanted a portrait of the woman. Then he said the woman had 'died' in the early part of the last war [World War I] when Mrs. Clarke was just under ten. The mother passed on in January, 1915; the child was nine years and five months old.

In a later telephone talk the artist gave a detailed description of the mother, talking of her emaciated face, deep-sunken eyes, and drawn mouth, the result of suffering. Yet, though he kept seeing this face, the artist said he wanted to draw a happy picture, with laughing mouth and eyes. This was the kind of picture for which Mrs. Clarke had longed, the picture from the Beyond. But of this Leah knew nothing at the time, but he did know that the mother did her hair in a bun. He had said so on the telephone, and he said so as he drew it in on the sketch, but the daughter denied it. So, the bun was taken out – and re-inserted again.

Leah was right, for Mrs. Clarke later found a picture of her mother, and to her great embarrassment and the delight of Leah, there was a bun. Also in the portrait is an earring, which though not shown in the 'bun' photograph is evidential, for Mrs. Clarke remembers that her mother sometimes wore them.

So, from small things like doing the hair in a bun and wearing earrings the evidence grows and, from beyond the chance of deception and error, the 'dead', bound only by the tie of affection, keep their pledge and maintain the link invisible but stronger than grief or pain.

The séance room is the great leveller – and the great dispeller of false ideas, of foolish prejudices. One visit to an evidential circle usually impresses the alert observer with at least the opinion that it is not a mutual admiration society, and that many things that could not be challenged here are criticised there without rancour, and do not leave a sense of resentment.

That observation comes out of my own experience, and is reinforced by what happened to Mrs. Louie Hill, a healing medium. She heard Frank Leah relay for her Spirit messages from her father who said he was strict about religious observances and that his daughter had spent many gloomy Sundays as a child. Mrs. Hill came to this evidence when she sought a portrait of her guide. Someone said she should try Leah, but she rejected the idea.

Two days later she was making jam when suddenly she imperilled the whole boiling by going to the telephone and calling up Leah. Straight to the point went Mrs. Hill. "I am Louie Hill," she said. "Can you see anything or anybody with me?" Leah was just as sharp, for he immediately described her guide. He said also that there was a relative with the guide, but Mrs. Hill did not ask about that, and Leah did not say who he was. The artist volunteered that if he was given an hour he would find out more about the two 'dead' people he had seen.

An hour later Mrs. Hill was on the telephone again, and was told by Leah: "Since you rang me I have had a long session with your father. He has been telling me all about your life and his life." Then followed the description, which Mrs. Hill recognised, and she also confirmed the statements about strict religious observance and the gloomy Sundays.

Leah reported, still on the telephone, that the 'dead' man was showing him a watch-chain "with a history". That struck a chord of memory, for when she was a little girl Mrs. Hill found a tiger's claw, which she gave to her father. When she went to work in a jeweller's shop, one of the first things she did with her small savings was to have the claw mounted in gold. This her father put on his watch-chain, which he wore every day until he left for the land where watch-chains are not required. So the tiger's claw returned to her. It was the only one of her father's possessions that she wanted.

All these facts were given over the telephone, and when Mrs. Hill called next day the artist showed her two sketches, one of her guide and one of her father. She recognised both. The guide she had seen often clairvoyantly, and the sketch, she said, resembled a painting of him done some time before.

Mrs. Hill's father continued to give her evidence, telling of the family's strong antipathy to Spiritualism. Then Leah was shown, from the Spirit World, a picture of the father taken when he was much younger. Mrs. Hill denied this, saying there was only one photograph of her father in existence, taken about three months before the end. Mrs. Hill visited Leah the following day, and in a few minutes he drew a life-like portrait. While he was doing this Leah experienced the sensations of the father's last illness.

In her bag Mrs. Hill had the photograph taken of her father three months before he 'died', and when she compared them she said: "It's Dad absolutely." When her husband saw the drawing he was so impressed that he stated: "It is an exact picture of him as he looked just before his passing. It is as if Leah knew him intimately."

Then Mr. Hill suggested that they compare it with another picture taken thirty years before he passed on. Only then did Mrs. Hill remember that she had the photograph which her father had shown clairvoyantly to Leah. So, again the artist was right – because he was reporting what was apparent to his psychic vision, whereas the sitter was relying on memory, which is not always faithful.

10

Two Sons Return to Mother

A mother went to Frank Leah to get the psychic portrait of one son who gave his life in a flight over Germany – and received instead the living likeness of another son who passed in the fighting in Burma. The mother is Mrs. M. S. Hollington, of Cranford Lane, Westbury-on-Trym, Bristol. She wrote to Leah asking for a sitting without saying why. Later she telephoned, and as you have read so often before, he began to give a description of her son, an airman, he said, with a long moustache for his twenty-one years.

He 'died', said the medium, in the first month of the war. His aeroplane was shot down. Mrs. Hollington said all the facts were as Leah stated. Then the mother visited the artist's London studio and before her eyes Leah lived again through the agonies of the young airman's passing. I have chronicled this often in this book, but you should try to realise what it means to feel the pains of another, pains you need not endure, but pains which must be endured in so many instances of the first return of those who have reached the shores of the promised land, for in their contact with this world they re-live their own experiences.

You ask: "Why?" The answer is that is the law. I did not make it, neither did any Spirit guide nor any medium. It is there. It happens that sensitives of the type of Leah pay a high price for the service they render to humanity. And all to dry away the tears of those who mourn because they love. Did any priest do so much, the world would ring with the story of the reproduction of the stigmata. But because a Spiritualist medium does it in the course of his work it is taken for granted. And there is always lurking behind the scenes the fetid provision of ancient Acts of Parliament that make such men outlaws and subject at the whim of any common informer – and how common they are – to prosecution for fortune-telling. Some day a procession of all those who have had proved to them the priceless gift of the Spirit will march to Parliament, and thence to the great abbey not far from it, to declare that no longer should a great nation shame itself by penalising those who perform so sacred a task.

Sometimes Leah suffers in detailed intensity every moment of the passing of men like young Hollington. And as his mother watched, the 'dead' airman said through Leah's lips: "I was shot down after a reconnaissance flight over Germany. My body fell out of the aeroplane with the others. My body was washed up on the shores of Germany nine weeks later." Then the artist went to his easel to draw the young man he saw and whose death story he had just told. In less than a minute the drawing was done – but it was not the face he had seen so clearly. In a life that is lived always in the unusual, Leah now had the strange experience of having his hand controlled.

With Mrs. Hollington was her daughter, and when she saw the portrait she said: "It's Bob," and the mother cried out: "You have got my other son." Leah was as surprised as the two visitors. Then he said: "This boy was alive in Burma three months ago. I hear Rangoon, Pegu, Prome." He said he was an officer in a county regiment. "That is true," said the mother. "He was reported dead, but I hoped he might be alive."

Leah explained that the fact that he had drawn the portrait in this abnormal way showed that this son had also passed over. The artist said also he was informed psychically that Mrs. Hollington was going elsewhere to find corroboration of this statement. This also was admitted, for the mother said she had an appointment with Estelle Roberts. She was asked not to say anything about her visit to the studio so as to make her next séance more evidential.

Three days later Leah, who had drawn one brother in a minute, had great difficulty in drawing the other whom he had seen so clearly.

All that Leah had said in his studio was confirmed at the Estelle Roberts séance. Though John Hollington had proved his Survival to his mother through this medium some time before her visit to Leah, Estelle Roberts knew nothing of the reason for this second visit. John was the first to manifest through the medium. He confirmed all that happened in Leah's studio, and explained how the artist came to draw his brother. He said: "I stood on one side to let my brother show himself. Bob is with me. He is very agitated." Then there were repeated the messages Mrs. Hollington received through Leah. As additional evidence to show that they were in his studio when the portrait of Bob was drawn, they told how he had hesitated before putting the pip on Bob's shoulder, and of the difficulty Leah had at first with the way John's hair was done at one side.

It's not all tears at séances. Usually when the tears are dried there is a laugh, and one came when one son asked his mother: "How did you like the portrait Leah showed you of his young lady?" Mrs. Hollington laughed at this recollection of her talk with Leah during which he showed her a picture of his 'young lady', a friend who is just a hundred years old.

Through Estelle Roberts, Bob Hollington made the definite statement that he 'died' in the Far East, and the mother was also told that she had received the psychic portraits of her two sons within four days. Then she produced these pictures, and although the medium had never seen the photographs, she said at once which was which.

Finally, Mrs. Hollington sent to *Psychic News* the Spirit drawings and the photographs for comparison, and wrote: "The photograph of Robert has not been seen at all by Mr. Leah. I have three grown-up sons who are very critical and sift all the evidence mainly because they hate the idea of me being deceived and led away by wishful thinking. They consider the drawings 100 per cent perfect.

"I have always been opposed to the idea of making public any psychic experience I have had through the loss of my two wonderful boys, but John told me to make it known for the sake of other mothers. After all, if I had not seen the other psychic drawings in *Psychic News* I should never have heard of Mr. Leah.

"I should like to express my gratitude for the consideration he showed me and for the great help he gave me. His information and descriptions were perfect."

Perhaps you are looking for the flaw in this account. Perhaps you think it odd that Mrs. Hollington went to two mediums. Before she went to the artist's studio she was a stranger to him, and in case you still have reservations and ask if Leah and Estelle Roberts knew one another and arranged it between them, the answer – apart from the fact that they could not have known what the mother did not know – is that the two mediums are strangers and have never met, even casually.

In Spiritualism one piece of evidence leads to another. When Arthur E. Smith, of Wolverhampton, saw in *Psychic News* the psychic drawing of Dr. Letari, the 'dead' Hindu doctor who heals through W. H. Lilley, it gave rise to this letter telling the story of his wife making a request for a sitting with Leah. This is Smith's letter: "Some time ago you may remember I made an application to you for the address of Mr. Frank Leah, the well-known psychic artist, and you were kind enough to pass the letter on to him for me. The request was from my wife who had passed into the Spirit two years before, this request being received through my daughter's automatic writing at the tea table while she and I were discussing your published drawing of Dr. Letari.

"Mr. Leah was kind enough to give me a sitting some time later, and although I have had sittings for various types of phenomena, I think this medium does give a more wonderful conception of mediumship than any other I have met so far. I do not disparage any other medium, but I definitely went for a drawing of my wife who is as real to me, and I realise, probably closer to me than at any time in our thirty-three years' acquaintance with one another, including twenty-four years of married life.

"I got my drawing all right from the artist, but, believe me, that before the artist had been long on the job the drawing had become secondary to the medium's philosophy and clairvoyance. A little difficulty was certainly caused by the excitement on the other side, and the drawing could not be finished on the first day. But as I was staying in London, I sat on the second and all was O.K., as can be judged by the enclosed copy of the drawing. As regards the medium's clairvoyance it was certainly wonderful leading off with the parting in the hair. Of course, that was a thing I could verify right off. With regard to the mouth, you will note that the photo has the lips slightly apart, but my wife always regarded this photo showing a very hard mouth and not her natural mouth. Her idea of this was certainly borne out by the Spirit drawing.

"With regard to the eyes, I do not think any mortal could be more real than the medium's drawing, for they are perfect. I am afraid I am one of those unobservant people who could live with a woman for ever and never know the colour of her eyes, but this was given to me by the medium, and was fully borne out by my wife's passport, which was issued in May 1939.

"I assure you, Mr. Editor, that no help was given to the artist by me, and I certainly denied some of the points in the clairvoyance, the chief of which was in the way my wife did her hair. I protested to the artist that she did not do her hair low down on the sides of her forehead, but he was certainly positive in what he knew. I think by the time he had finished he must have thought I was barmy, for I certainly gave him no help. His mediumship proved 100 per cent correct on every little detail, as you can judge for yourself from the enclosed copies of the psychic photograph and the original photograph.

"Please do not think that I went to Frank Leah for proof, I did not. I went at the specific request of my wife from Spirit for a drawing to be made of her by Frank Leah, the same to be hung in her own home. She told me from Spirit that she had not at all altered in the two years since she had passed over, and that she was more alive than ever she had been on earth. She has given me on many occasions the cause of her physical death, and this was fully borne out by Frank Leah."

Nobody could know better than Mr. Smith whether it was his wife, and even when he forgot the colour of her eyes, her passport supported the medium. These are facts from which you cannot escape.

"Too wonderful to be true." That is what Vera Jeffries, of Augustus Road, Wimbledon Park, south-west London, said of the Frank Leah portrait of her friend, H. Wharton-Wells, B.Mus., F.R.C.O., L.R.A.M. She said so when he spoke to her in the direct voice at a sitting to which Mrs. Jeffries was invited by a friend. Leslie Flint, the medium for the direct voice, was on a short leave from the Army, and so could not give many séances. His guide introduced Wharton-Wells, who addressed her, saying that she doubted the picture, but it was he. And she answered that it was a fact that she had doubted, for "it was too wonderful to be true."

By way of additional evidence, the musician said his friend had nine photographs of him in her bag, and "one other thing of mine." He was right, for the 'other thing' was a gold pencil.

Now this is how it began. Wharton-Wells had known Mrs. Jeffries and her husband for many years. About twelve years ago he went to live with them, and became almost one of the family. Mrs. Jeffries is a Spiritualist, and tried to interest him. But he had orthodox views on religion. He was then organist of Putney Parish Church. But one day his son was suddenly taken ill and there was an immediate operation in hospital. That was in the afternoon. At 6.45 the same day he rallied and said clearly:

"They are coming for me at a quarter-to-twelve." The nurse said: "Don't worry. He is delirious." Despite her opinion, the young man passed at exactly a quarter to twelve, and the first breach was made in the father's orthodoxy.

About three months later he visited his son's grave in Buckinghamshire, accompanied by Vera Jeffries, who placed some asters on the grave. This was not mentioned to anyone. The next day Wharton-Wells and Vera Jeffries were at a séance when the son materialised, approached his father and said: "Hello, Father. Thank Vera for the asters. I was with you at the grave yesterday."

Then the father began to study Spiritualism, and the conviction he reached of its truth stayed with him until he passed in May, 1942. Nine months before he 'died' he wrote: "After I have left this sphere I will try to come to you." He succeeded so well that Vera Jeffries thought it 'too wonderful to be true,' and this is how it happened.

Some time ago Vera Jeffries had an urge to telephone Leah, and though she had heard a good deal of him, they had not met. Neither had the medium met Wharton-Wells. There and then on the telephone Leah described the musician, saying he was "an academic man, who had been in the public eye and connected with the Church". Among the physical points given were the moustache and beard which, said the medium, used to be longer and dark brown. That was confirmed by Vera Jeffries. When she went to the artist's studio the following day she saw the completed portrait. The likeness was amazing to her, and Leah said that he had the impression that the man he had drawn wanted to speak to her in the direct voice. You have already read that he did so.

In the home of Vera Jeffries there was a picture which Wharton-Wells never liked. He promised to give her a photograph to fit the frame. Frank Leah's portrait of him fits the frame exactly. The fitting of the picture to the frame may be coincidence, but nothing else in this case could be so explained, for it all weaves together into the pattern of evidence drawn by the hands of those who return to prove that they are not 'dead'.

11
This Truth is Growing

There are many who sneer at Spiritualism, and, of course, at Spiritualists, as being ignorant men and women and, pointing the finger of scorn at them, say they have never produced any work of art, have written nothing that can be called literature, nor, it is alleged, have they invented anything of lasting worth to the world. The answer, in part, is that Spiritualists are ordinary men and women who after investigation and thought on facts observed become – Spiritualists. They believe in demonstrated Survival after death as opposed to those who have a hazy conception based on a few references in scriptures. So any man or woman, be they high or low, intellectual or merely one of those who make the world comfortable for others, is likely to become a Spiritualist. You never can tell when you will be convinced, but you can always tell when you will not be convinced – by refusing in advance to allow your judgment to be moved by facts.

Therefore, it is not surprising that Spiritualism grows, and that there are Spiritualists wherever there are men and women free to inquire. There are many who prefer their names not to be revealed, for reasons best known to themselves, though I cannot think of any reason to prevent anyone acknowledging what is true and of the very greatest help to humanity. Still, that is for individual decision, and when those who might well have an excuse for not revealing their conviction do so, we are proud to mention it. When anyone in the public eye becomes, say, a convert to Rome, it is reported in the Roman Catholic Press, and often in other papers, too. I have not heard that it goes against them, or that it is supposed to show any sign of lack of judgement. But there are many who have sat in the séance room and welcomed their 'dead' relatives and friends. Yet we are asked to keep it quiet – for the present. The present soon becomes the past, and it is forgotten, and the value of the testimony of one more person is lost.

I always object to such secrecy – unless there is a reason beyond the personal, or one that is likely to harm others. Yet I still think it wrong to hide a truth, and withhold the recognition to this work that it rightly deserves. Therefore, while the number of Spiritualists grows, so also does the total of secret believers. We no longer live in the Dark Ages – although we do live in the black-out ages – and if it were not for the struggles of those who never shunned publicity – and sometimes had to court it to make their voices heard – the world would know little today of the only common platform on which all nations can meet – Spiritualism.

You have read here so far of people of all classes who have had their grief assuaged by the touch of the Spirit. I have tried to make the case as wide as possible by telling again the stories of people such as we all know receiving the facts that compelled them to admit that those they love live beyond the grave. There are others who withheld their evidence, while accepting its truth. But it would not add to the purpose of this work to name them and start a controversy on the reasons for secrecy. Those who ask most, for the publication of the fact that they live, are the 'dead'. They are the most insistent. Mostly the insistence comes from those who in this life either denied the fact of Survival or had not investigated. Because they have become painfully aware of the loss caused by ignorance they return to comfort those left behind – and to spread the knowledge that enabled them to do so.

It may sound simple as I put it – I hope it is – but it becomes complicated in the hands of many people who begin to see reasons why they alone should keep their stories dark. Abraham Lincoln was a practising Spiritualist and could not understand why there should be any discussion of it; he merely said that the reports of his séances were only half the facts. But Queen Victoria – who with the Highland ghillie, John Brown, as her permanent medium, spoke every week to Prince Albert – did not publish the fact, and her diaries were destroyed.

There is concealment in high places, and it is against this secrecy that Leah has often protested. He is an artist and a medium, and he expects that when he has given his services – often for a small return – that those who are so delighted in his studio will be equally delighted to let the facts be known. The truth never hurts in the long run, and if those who are persuaded that this is true feel that they will suffer some opposition because they are honest, then they are in the very best company, for that is the natural and universal experience of all who tread in new ways.

Here is one who did not hide behind position; Dr. Margaret Vivian who, like all of us, has to earn her living. There is as much prejudice in the medical profession as anywhere against Spiritualism, but she has recorded her experiences, and was the medium through whom a fine Spiritualist book was produced. Her guide is a young British officer who was killed during the South African War. His identity was proved through several mediums, including the psychic photographer, John Myers.

When Dr. Vivian went to Leah she was, as were all the others, a stranger, yet working in the dark, he produced these three striking drawings. Her father was a parson, who avoided wearing the 'dog' collar, and for evidential purposes he shows it in the right-hand corner. Though he wore glasses, as this sketch shows, Dr. Vivian has no photograph of him wearing them. The drawing of her mother is a life-like piece of portraiture.

If you say you doubt these drawings, then you have to challenge the whole work, for the comparative photographs always show the basic resemblance, though, of course, no one with any perception of the value of an artist's work would expect photographic reproduction in normal work. There is another name for that. But the point I make is this – that if a non-psychic artist makes an individual interpretation of a sitter it is hailed; therefore when the 'dead' – the living 'dead' – pose for Leah he is seeing not what you might expect, but a vibrant personality who comes with a purpose. The 'dead' co-operate as the living never can. They can suggest what features are under-portrayed or overdone, and they help with the small points of personality that they know will be recognition for their relatives. Therefore, in assessing the purely technical aspects of this work, it is as well to bear this in mind. Each portrait has a history, each has a message, and it is that the 'dead' live on.

One of the heroes of the raid on the German naval base at St. Nazaire on the French Atlantic coast returned to his father and posed for his portrait in Leah's studio. The young man, whose name is not given, because at the time of writing this account the father was still inquiring into Spiritualism and wished to keep his name secret, was a naval lieutenant. The *London Gazette*, describing the action which earned him mention in despatches, referred to his "dauntless devotion to duty at the forward gun of the motor-launch which led the port column...quite unprotected in the face of intense fire at close range he showed unshaken coolness until he was killed at his post."

But that was not the end. His father came up to London and telephoned to Frank Leah for an appointment. As they were talking the artist described the young lieutenant. In his studio the next day the artist 'roughed' in the head and in his letter describing his evidence the father writes: "Even at this stage I could see my son's likeness." A few days later the father sat with the medium, Annie Brittain, and through her his son communicated. The medium referred to the portrait by talking of "a sketch you have that has pleased you". When the portrait was completed and the father had gone home, he wrote of it: "It is a wonderful portrait. I and others who knew my son well consider it an inspired piece of work, a better portrait than any photograph

I have of him. It is a wonderful work, and has brought comfort to my son's wife and myself and others who knew and cared for him."

The young lieutenant and Leah had never met in this world. He came from another world to comfort those he loved. You can gauge his character, and that he would be anxious to return, from this extract from a letter which he left when he went away on active duty:

"Dear Dad – By the time you get this you will know the news. Please don't lose heart. You know there is a life hereafter, and I am certain of it. Life is just a passing phase, and although it seems so long, it is really only a short interval in eternity. Please try and be cheerful, and try to keep my wife's spirits up. Please remember that I died, I hope, that the world might be a better place."

And it is in that hope also, that this book has been written.

You may have read Oscar Wilde's famous story, *The Picture of Dorian Gray*, in which the living portrait changes. Now here is the story of a fact – the psychic portrait of a great medium – William Hope, the Spirit photographer, of Crewe, which was transformed as two people watched. One was Frank Leah, the artist; the other was Betty Shaw. This is her story.

She had a sitting with Hope, taking with her a packet of sealed photographic plates. She opened the packet in the dark room, initialled the plates, and loaded the camera. Three photographs were taken, and of the two clear psychic extras which appeared she recognised one.

After Hope 'died' Betty Shaw says he returned to her through three mediums. Then she desired to have a picture of her guide, and asked Leah to do it. He was to her what he was to the others – a stranger. Thomas Wyatt, another medium, agreed to sit with them to provide extra power. Then the séance began. Wyatt was in trance. As so often happens, Leah was in pain, not his own, but the pain of another returning to this world.

They were in the dark when Leah said to Betty Shaw: "Over where your face must be, there is the face of a man so well illuminated that I must draw him." The artist then touched her face and described in detail the face he had seen superimposed on it. He switched on his torch, which gives a dim red light, and drew rapidly. Betty Shaw was anxious to see her guide, and when the features grew on the board she exclaimed: "Why, that's Billy." Leah said sharply; "Don't give me any names."

Betty Shaw had met Hope. Leah had not, but both stood and watched this amazing happening. She describes it: "As I watched the drawing, without the artist's hand touching it, we both noticed that the features were altering. They took on an expression of extreme suffering."

The portrait took about seven minutes to draw, and when the lights were put on Betty Shaw produced a photograph of Hope that she always carried with her. No one knew this, and she says: "The difference between this photograph and Leah's charcoal portrait is that my photograph is full face and wearing a cap, while the drawing shows him three-quarter view without headgear. The likeness is quite unquestionable."

Wyatt's guide said, before the lights were turned on, that the Spirit people were pleased with a most successful experiment, and at a later sitting, when Leah asked why he, who knew nothing of Hope, should have been chosen in this unusual fashion to do his portrait, he was given this answer: "When we looked for means of vindicating this great warrior who has suffered so much persecution in his work for us, even since he came over, we sought the one means of proving his features through a source independent of photography. That's why we chose you. We wanted Billy's features to be given through a pencil – through a medium who had no knowledge whatever of them. By doing so, we have accomplished our object. He has given incontestable proof of his Survival."

So does the Spirit World regard its warriors, the men and women who lift the load from the heart of the world. As Hope has brought incontestable proof of Survival to thousands, I hope you are convinced that this story of the mediumship of Frank Leah has done the same. It is the reason for his life and work, and he asks no other recommendation.

This is the only case of its kind, one in which the psychic artist, after doing a portrait, co-operated in modelling a bust so lifelike that the son, who started by being an anti-Spiritualist, was deeply affected by the result. It all began when Mrs. Harold Richardson, of South Carolina, an American married to a Canadian, called on Leah for a sitting during which he did a rough sketch in two-and-a-half minutes. The drawing turned out to be of a striking old man with a beard. His shoulders had a pronounced slope, and the head an unusual shape. When the sitter, the 'dead' man's daughter-in-law, had gone, Leah called on a sculptor friend, A.J. Stevenson, who asked Leah if he had had any new experiences. Leah said he had drawn a very unusual head, and after describing it, he made two rapid drawings. The sculptor said he was sure the artist had got the shape of the shoulders and the back of the head wrong. But, after some discussion, they modelled the bust in clay in conformity with Leah's description.

Now, the artist knew nothing of the sitter's husband, apart from his name and the fact that he was antagonistic to Spiritualism. So, when he called at the Richardsons' hotel to show the picture he had drawn, Richardson said: "What do you want? I cannot see you." Leah answered that he wanted nothing except to show the picture, and when he did so the man who was antagonistic to Spiritualism exclaimed: "Why, that is my father." His father was Archdeacon Richardson, D.D., of Huron Diocese, Ontario, who was also well-known in the United States as a preacher. When the son asked why his father should show himself, Leah said it was because he was concerned about his health, indicating that the son suffered from stomach trouble. Richardson at first denied there was anything wrong. Then he admitted that he had suffered a lot from some internal trouble. He was so impressed that he arranged to meet the artist at the sculptor's studio two days later to see the bust. Before he arrived Leah asked the odd-job man to go to Woolworth's for a pair of pince-nez, telling him that if he did not hurry he would not get them. The man came back surprised at Leah's 'inside information' about the state of the pince-nez market at Woolworth's – for he had bought the last pair. When Richardson saw the completed bust, with the pince-nez, he again expressed his amazement. After his surprise was over and he had admired the work, Richardson gave Leah a letter saying that all the statements made by him were accurate. He also thought the bust was so good that he decided to have it cast.

Later, when the sculptor compared the bust with drawings and photographs of the 'dead' man, he admitted his error, and said that Leah had been right about the shape of the head, and also the abnormal slope of the shoulders. The photographs were sent from America by the wife, who, in an enthusiastic letter, told how she and her husband had received confirmation of the archdeacon's Survival at a direct-voice séance. Not only did Richardson's father and mother speak to them, but five others did so as well, and both father and son were so joyful that they wept.

Spiritualism is for all men and women, for all races and for all times. It matters not how humble you are, nor does it gain you any preference if you are what the world calls powerful. The only claim to this knowledge is that you seek it, and in proportion to your real need, and in proportion to your sincerity and earnestness, it is given in the right conditions and at the right time. This truth is something you cannot lose; it cannot be argued away; it cannot be legislated out of existence, although in darker times in the world's not far-distant history mediums have been burned at the stake or driven from the lands they sought to serve.

The only thing wrong with Spiritualism is that there is not enough of it, and that is because there are too few mediums. But that is something humanity can remedy by finding among its hundreds of millions the relatively small army of those who are willing to be trained as instruments of the Spirit. It is true that the psychic organism has to be there, but that is soon discovered and simply developed. It but remains to unfold the faculties and test the character, and then a great work begins, a work that begets such a book as this, which even though you may consider it indifferently written, nevertheless presents the evidence.

Frankly, we Spiritualists are propagandists in the very best sense of that much-derided term – for we seek to spread what we know to be true in the interests of our fellow men. We have no other cause to serve. There are no fortunes in this cause. There is little glory to be won, and there is much hard work, often in the silence and obscurity of the places where only the pioneer flourishes. To hear someone say: "It is true. I have proved it," – that is the reward we seek. In the train of that conviction there follows a series of acts which must either place you on the road of evolution of the spiritual man – or you have failed to perceive the light that shines through these facts.

This is a great and solemn work, though we do not weigh down the spirits of those we approach with the heaviness of orthodox religions. It is solemn, for it treats of the very basis of life itself, because it touches the well-spring of human thought and will and action; and it is great for it touches every facet of life and leaves none unchanged.

Yet it is with joy that we move towards the first century of our service to mankind, a century in which no infamy has been left unexploited to demean our purpose and falsify our facts. To their lasting shame those who should have welcomed our message with gladness were the first to cast stones. But time has taken its revenge, and those who sought to place the mark of falsehood upon the brow of this movement are themselves neglected, shorn of their former power, and now seeking desperately a way in which to redeem their fortunes. It is too late. The tide has gone, and with it the argosy of their hopes of world domination.

Now a new day dawns, a day long planned by those who

from the Spirit World always have stretched forth the hand of friendship to any who would enlist in the task of raising the scales from the eyes of mankind. The former potentates of this world are weak; the tyrants, religious and political, are declining; and from the ruins of the old world the new will be built. It is for this that Spiritualism was born, it is for this that its mission has been organised; it is for the inspiring of all men that the mediums, the writers, the healers, the speakers have laboured.

When the soul of man slept long in the dark night of this world the agents of the Spirit did not rest. Long and late they laboured that our burden should be lightened. It was not they who made the slums, who devised the creeds that produce slums of the mind; not they who decreed poverty for the many and privilege for the few. They are the helpers of all men and all movements that seek to lift the burden which is our common lot. They earnestly desire a newer, better world because they know from experience that persistence of the old means universal disaster, and the passing away of not only the bad but all the hard-earned good with it.

For that purpose, then, this Spiritualism was brought into being. And Spiritualism will remain and grow until its influence has so lifted and refined the human consciousness that death will lose its fear and fear will lose its hold on the mind; until the human heart beats in the security of knowledge that beyond this life there is a greater life for which this is but a preparation. But to live and to tarry purposelessly until the day of release comes would be to fall into the error that has cursed so many civilisations before. We are to be free to live, and to live life to the full in all its planes and spheres. The purpose of our dwelling here is to evolve character that we may pass more rapidly into fuller existence when we lay aside the physical body.

That is the beginning. The glorious end no man may see. Enough work lies to the hand of every one to exhaust all our energies in all our lifetimes. Let us begin with the example before us of one medium who is loyal to his task, for only by loyalty can we achieve this religious duty of spreading a truth that can, in time, set all men free from their fears and wants. The work one man can do is little, but when the power of the Spirit is added to it, the increase is a hundredfold.

Leah is one faithful medium; there are many, and as the century of our endeavour approaches, there will be many more, and soon the world will be aware that the great truth that began as a tiny seed has grown into a mighty oak.

oooOooo

Lightning Source UK Ltd.
Milton Keynes UK
UKHW02f0804301117
313588UK00004B/227/P